Narrative Con/Texts in *Dubliners*

Narrative Con/Texts in *Dubliners*

Bernard Benstock

University of Illinois Press
Urbana and Chicago

Manufactured in Hong Kong

C   5   4   3   2   1

This book is printed on acid-free paper.

Library of Congress Cataloging-in-Publication Data
Benstock, Bernard.
Narrative con/texts in *Dubliners* / Bernard Benstock.
p.   cm.
Includes index.
ISBN 0–252–02058–8 (alk. paper)
1. Joyce, James, 1882–1941. *Dubliners*. 2. Dublin (Ireland) in
literature. 3. Narration (Rhetoric) I. Title. II. Title:
Narrative contexts in *Dubliners*.
PR6019.09D867   1994
823'.912—dc20   93–3377
                                                       CIP

To Shari
who doubles as "distant music"
and with thanks again to
Belinda Ghitis and Zack Bowen

Contents

Acknowledgements

Earlier versions of parts of the various chapters have appeared in the following books and journals, and I express my gratitude to their editors: *Journal of Modern Literature, Twentieth Century Literature, L'Herne, Abiko Literary Quarterly, Rivista de Letterature Moderne e Comparate, James Joyce Quarterly, Southern Review, Modern Fiction Studies, Twentieth Century Literary Criticism* and *The Languages of Joyce.*

I also want to acknowledge my appreciation to the Camargo Foundation in Cassis, France, where early segments of these chapters were written.

A Note on the Text

References to *Dubliners* are to the 1961 Viking Press edition edited by Robert Scholes. Quotations are by page numbers from that edition, with the title of the individual story indicated as follows:

Si	The Sisters
En	An Encounter
Ar	Araby
Ev	Eveline
Af	After the Race
Tw	Two Gallants
Bo	The Boarding House
Li	A Little Cloud
Co	Counterparts
Cl	Clay
Pa	A Painful Case
Iv	Ivy Day in the Committee Room
Mo	A Mother
Gr	Grace
De	The Dead

References to *Ulysses* are the 1986 Random House edition edited by Hans Walter Gabler. Quotations are by inclusive line numbers from that edition, with the chapter titles indicated as follows:

Te	Chapter 1, Telemachus
Ne	Chapter 2, Nestor
Pr	Chapter 3, Proteus
Ca	Chapter 4, Calypso
Lo	Chapter 5, Lotus Eaters
Ha	Chapter 6, Hades
Ae	Chapter 7, Aeolus
Le	Chapter 8, Lestrygonians
SC	Chapter 9, Scylla and Charybdis
WR	Chapter 10, Wandering Rocks
Si	Chapter 11, Sirens

Cy	Chapter 12, Cyclops
Na	Chapter 13, Nausicaa
OS	Chapter 14, Oxen of the Sun
Ci	Chapter 15, Circe
Eu	Chapter 16, Eumaeus
It	Chapter 17, Ithaca
Pe	Chapter 18, Penelope

References to *Finnegans Wake* (FW) are to the 1947 edition (New York: Viking Press), incorporating the author's "Corrections of Misprints". Quotations are by page and inclusive line numbers.

References to *A Portrait of the Artist as a Young Man* (AP) are to the 1964 edition (New York: Viking Press) edited by Chester G. Anderson. Quotations are by page number from that edition.

References to *Stephen Hero* (SH) are from the 1963 edition (New York: New Directions) edited by Theodore Spencer. Quotations are by page number from that edition.

Note regarding ellipses: those ellipses which are part of the text being quoted are indicated by closely spaced ellipses (...), whereas deletions made by the author are marked by normally spaced ellipses (. . .).

Introduction:
A Confluence of Texts

*But total context is unmasterable, both in principle and in practice.
Meaning is context-bound, but context is boundless.*
Jonathan Culler

James Joyce's *Dubliners* has eluded critical classification because it
remains a "sampling" of experiences within discrete borders (fifteen
separate short stories), as well as a "running text" that forms a con-
secutive whole (a single work of interconnected entities). When
"Araby" is anthologized in a volume of works by various authors
(as it often is), the assumption is that it can stand on its own as a
total experience, and the final reactions of the boy narrator derive
from his immediate disappointment regarding Mangan's sister, the
darkened bazaar, and his insufficient funds (although it may then
take on the contextual possibilities of the anthology – one of *Irish*
stories, for example). When read inside *Dubliners* as the third story
of childhood experiences, that resolution can also be read as a
cumulative reaction to the boy's traumas that include a succession
of events such as a priest's death and a frightening encounter with a
stranger. We are constantly aware that the barriers exist between
each of the fifteen stories, but never sure how firm those barriers
actually are, of what seeps through to create a "Dubliners" context
in lieu of an individual context. James Duffy stands resolute as an
individuated self, attempting to divorce himself from Dublin and
from almost all other Dubliners, yet his very isolation dooms him to
identifying with others around him, the fornicators in the park –
hardly his normal context.

The notion of context serves as a portal of entry into the narrat-
ive(s) of *Dubliners*, the way in which narrative discourse implicitly
binds itself while simultaneously failing to contain that which it
would attempt to define. Reading contextually means following the
implications of its double sense (of context and con/text) through a
series of critical distinctions (either/or, neither/nor, both/and) that
mark the particular double bind of Joyce's narratives. The critical
effort to define the exact nature of a particular instance, to locate

1

the source or allusion or historical identity, attempts to fix a single reality onto the text, "closing in" the context irrevocably, yet each of these efforts is far more valuable in expanding the possibilities of a multiple text, in keeping with the already dual nature of the tightly bound tales within the boundlessness of the outer structure. *Dubliners* continues to exist, not as a completed or abandoned work of literary art, but as an expanding document of lives in the process of being lived, a "work in progress".

What constitutes contextualization in a Joycean text, especially one that is both highly selective and all-inclusive in its content? Irish political history, Joyce's personal experiences, the byproducts of Joyce's education and reading, previous versions of the same narrative, all serve as major repositories, while internal aspects of each of the tales contribute to extended aspects of the others, both in sequential progression and in retrospective reaction. Whereas *Dubliners* (and *A Portrait of the Artist as a Young Man*) provide pre-texts for *Ulysses*, the process has possibilities in reverse as well, to read *Dubliners* through *Ulysses* (and *Finnegans Wake*). Joyce "accepted" the applicability of the Russo-Finnish War to *Finnegans Wake*, despite the fact that that work-in-progress was already in print, since the war corroborated the shooting of the Russian General – by a Finn. The *Wake* contains the splitting of the atom and the successful utilization of television, although both of those phenomena took place after Joyce's death: they existed in the 1930s as distinct possibilities that Joyce (nightly) possibilized.

The laws of probability have long since been ratified, but those of possibility usually exist outside the framework of the literary text, when the text presumably has its locus in some sort of accepted realistic frame. That Maria will be flustered enough by the politeness of the gentleman on the tram to forget her plumcake is more than highly probable, and that his attentiveness derives from the aura of well-being induced by drink is so probable as to be assumed as inevitable (Joe Donnelly's hospitable offers of drinks to Maria provide one inner context, while the behaviour of the uncle in "Araby" provides an "outer" one). Yet what are the extended possibilities of Maria's hold on life as a related consequence of her encounter on the tram? The uncle contributes to the boy's ultimate disappointment as much as the colonel-looking gentleman does to Maria's and in each story the closure suggests a closing off of poss-ibilities for the protagonist as a result of the experience. Characters in *Dubliners* who are extended into *Ulysses* bring with them their

original contextual baggage, which upon inspection reveals aspects
that elucidate their situations in the originating texts. Characters
who do not make the transition into *Ulysses* then exist within the
realm of multiple possibilities as products of open-ended resolution. In both cases the "limitations" set on characterization by the
singular component of individuality may also be elusive; just as the
nameless boy of the first three stories evolves into the possibility of
three characters, James Flynn and James Duffy and James Doyle
(and even James Lennon) may have contextually suspect aspects of
each other, and each of them may prove to be more than the total of
their individual parts, putting the concept of individuality itself
into suspicion.

Each of Joyce's works contains its own critical apparatus contained in its own critical vocabulary to greater or lesser degrees –
and degrees of seriousness. None highlights its critical context
as flagrantly as *Dubliners*, where the time-honoured trinity of
paralysis–simony–gnomon declares itself on the first page of the
first story and trails its clouds of glory through the literary criticism
of the entire book, almost insistent on its constant reapplication.
The exalted prominence of this threesome tends to conceal various
other such devices, enough of them present throughout to provide
every reader of *Dubliners* with his or her individual methods of
investigation. In "Grace", for example, during a presumably casual
discussion on Pope Leo XIII, Martin Cunningham mentions that
His Holiness had written poetry in Latin:

– Is that so? said Mr Fogarty.
   Mr M'Coy tasted his whisky contentedly and shook
his head with a double intention, saying:
– That's no joke, I can tell you.   (Gr 167)

M'Coy's "double intention" seems to be a signifier in search of a
context. We are aware that everything the triumvirate of Cunningham, Power and M'Coy say in front of Kernan has its ulterior purpose of decoying him into the retreat, so that nothing they are
saying has a single intention (Fogarty has no idea of the greater
intentionality and plays his part inadvertently, and as inadvertently
gets swept into participation at the retreat). But double-inten-
tionality is by nature a two-edged sword, in this case suggesting
wide applicability to the ulterior purpose while calling attention to
M'Coy at the moment of double intention, where whisky and con-

tentment and the Pope's Latin poetry are a web of contextual possibilities. Does the duality lie in the position of Fogarty within the
construct or in M'Coy's double meaning regarding the difficulty of
writing poetry in Latin? Several possibilities remain open, and as
one falls away it is replaced by another, preventing the usurpation
by any single meaning, the "double intention" always suspect of
double intention. Even the title of the story exists simultaneously
on several levels: the grace of God that provides a state of grace
(ostensibly for Tom Kernan) is parodied by secular grace and
graciousness (especially Fogarty's), but the colloquialism that
begins "By the grace of God there goes . . ." plays its game of
double identity and concealment, revealing the gap between the
actual and the possible, the intersubstitution of one individual for
another. And, after all, Kernan's fall down the lavatory steps was
not fatal – by the grace of God.

The handful of characters in the *Dubliners* tales find themselves
carrying the excessive burden of representing a much larger
contingent than themselves, a composite population of Dubliners,
which, although it must necessarily fall short of the entire populace,
none the less is an interactive cross-section – within important class
limits. In various ways each is an actor who not only plays his or
her own role, but various other roles as well, as each of the characters takes on each other's roles. What every person is responsible
for within the circumstances of specific events often remains vague,
the extent of Farrington's villainy, for example, or Jimmy Doyle's
culpability in losing so much of the family fortune. Once we arrive
at a direct verdict of possible guilt, during the inquest into the
death of Emily Sinico, the ambiguous possibilities open up, and
spread back and forth across the fifteen stories. The Deputy Coroner's declaration that "No blame attached to anyone" (Pa 115) is
both accurate and misleading: he has no idea of the existence of
James Duffy or of the involvement of any "external" figure in the
case. The verdict of accidental death may be intended primarily to
mask a suspicion of suicide; the urging of "the railway company to
take strong measures to prevent the possibility of similar accidents
in the future" (Pa 115) shifts the focus on to the surface event rather
than any underlying causes. Duffy takes no solace from the verdict,
since he does not consider himself as a part of the all-embracing
population of "anyone", but obviously does blame himself even as
he attempts to exonerate himself: "He had no difficulty now in
approving of the course he had taken" (Pa 116). That course runs as
straight as a railway track to the events of the death.

"A Painful Case" is the only story in *Dubliners* where the word "blame" appears – and it does so four times. The setting up of a legal tribunal necessitates dealing with guilt and innocence, the process of indicting or exonerating. The railway company denies that it was in any way to blame, and the jury corroborates this version by deciding that the engine driver was not to blame – followed by the Deputy Coroner's overall dismissal of culpability. That "No blame attached to anyone" leaves blame unattached and in constant flux, allowing it to float freely in search of someone to attach itself to, and James Duffy consequently comes into "accidental" contact with the floating accusation: "He had done what seemed to him best. How was he to blame?" (Pa 116). Yet in its free flight it attaches itself to him regardless of his rationalization, although no finger pointed directly at it – as at the end of *Hamlet*. When Laertes declares that "the King's to blame", he is both direct and disingenuous, since he himself is certainly responsible for Hamlet's death, as much as Claudius. Laertes at this point takes the "larger" view, bringing the indirect culprit into the picture, and thereby diminishing if not completely masking his immediate role. Even when blame is so obviously attached, the position of the one making the accusation is ambiguous. Hamlet already knows that Claudius is to blame, and has for a long time, but now learns of the "accidentals" of Laertes' envenomed sword, the immediate instrument. Like the testifying James Lennon, Laertes is the engine driver who attempts to exonerate himself.

The extent to which every human being is responsible for his or her behaviour is often mitigated by inadvertence, accidentals, multiple involvements and lack of awareness. It is invariably tempting to attribute some element of sudden self-awareness to Joe Donnelly's tears, to assume that somehow the floating concept of blame has at this moment attached itself to him and that he will somehow face his real responsibilities toward Maria, but we must also remain aware that Mrs Donnelly has no such cognition of her role as the instrument of Maria's unfortunate condition and still exists as a deterrent to any ameliorization. In *Ulysses* the shifting of the burden of responsibility/culpability is operative throughout, both Stephen and Molly at odd instances assuming themselves to be blameless ("And the blame? As I am. As I am" – Pr 452; "small blame to me if I am a harumscarum" – Pe 1469–70), and Bloom of course is munificent in considering others to be without blame: "Can't blame them after all with the job they have" (Le 421–2). But what reverberates most potently throughout *Ulysses* is the even more remote concept of individual blamelessness that originates in Haines's bland assertion that "It seems history is to blame" (Te 649). Haines's concept reasserts itself at three later instances in Stephen's mind, despite his ambivalent relationship to history, that nightmare from which he is "trying to awake" (Ne 377) and later realizes that he "will never awake" (Ae 678). Irish history is a net flung at the souls of all of the participants in the activities of *Ulysses* and *Dubliners*, and the degree to which history is to blame is constantly active and ambiguous in their sense of their own involvement in the course of each other's lives. A shifting context, rather than a fixed reality, is operative in these texts, where the personal and the historical, the intentional and the accidental, the direct and the indirect, work against each other as on a shuttle loom, to complicate the weave and expand the scene "as on some vague arras" (AP 167).

The interweaving of the realistic and the symbolic is part of the continuous process, rather than two fixed aspects that co-exist in the nature of the narratives. Where an ostensibly realistic structure dominates the action, as in "A Painful Case", the operative confronter of that "reality" is the vague, almost ethereal hermit, James Duffy, and where the muted symbolic (what Stephen Dedalus had classified as "the supreme quality of beauty being a light from some other world" – AP 213) transfuses the narrative, as in "The Dead", the detailing observer is the hard-headed Gabriel Conroy. That each sees himself as a "man of letters" attests to their failings as literary artists, each only aware of half of the literary construct. Duffy's idealism had moved him for a time into active participation in the Irish Socialist Party, but what sent him into retreat "were hard-featured realists" who logically occupied that political terrain, and who (rather unrealistically) "resented an exactitude which was the product of a leisure not within their reach" (Pa 111). Gabriel, on the other hand, has been cutting a hard-featured course through the vague terrain of the Morkans' musical atmosphere, holding on to an exactitude when he "wanted to say that literature was above politics" (De 188). Yet when he finds himself confronting "grace and mystery" in Gretta's pose as she listens to the singing of "The Lass of Aughrim", he assumes that she is "a symbol of something". Determining that the proper format here would be a painting to be titled *Distant Music* (De 210) now removes him from the "presence" of the music that was his operative frame of reference, which he thought he could deal with by ignoring it, as with Mary Jane's Academy piece. The "real" piece of music that he had dismissed as outside the world that he diligently controls comes back to haunt him in the symbolic mysticism of Bartell D'Arcy's song, despite his attempt at "distancing". "Hard-featured realists" and "Distant Music" are co-ordinating factors in *Dubliners*, where cerebration and emotional reaction are in constant interaction, displacing and confronting each other.

Like Narrative Con/Texts in Ulysses (1991), *Narrative Con/Texts in Dubliners* is not a seamless critical construct, but a series of essays revised and augmented to suggest various approaches to the Joycean text. The first four chapters avoid any semblance of the sequential arrangements of the stories in favour of isolating pockets of conceptually arranged materials from the various tales in *Dubliners*. These are presented in terms of the narrative strategies operative throughout, the gnomonic structures, the symbolic characteristics, and the economic conditions governing the Dublin under scrutiny. The last two chapters, however, appear to return to a progressive treatment of the developing process in *Dubliners*, but even here certain liberties are taken in moving back and forth between stories not contiguous to each other in the sequence, reopening the possibilities of *Dubliners* as a work in constant progress that folds back on itself for greater amplification. Many of the same instances are returned to in each of the chapters in a criss-crossing pattern of cross-hatching, not to capture ultimate and conclusive explications but to reiterate the possibilities in Joyce's shifting contextualization.

1
Narrative Strategies: The Teller in the *Dubliners* Tale

Messenger took out his matchbox thoughtfully and lit his cigar.
I have often thought since on looking back over that strange time
that it was that small act, trivial in itself, that striking of that
match, that determined the whole aftercourse of both our lives.
Ulysses (Ae 762–5)

Those two sentences, neatly tucked away in the newspaper chapter of *Ulysses*, have only a tangential existence in that novel, a momentary construction in the mind of Stephen Dedalus during the "False lull" (Ae 761) in which J. J. O'Molloy lights his cigarette in preparation for his recitation. Disembodied as this fragment is – without prior or subsequent existence and no existing frame of reference – it represents a piece of literary narrative that makes itself significant through what it forecasts more than what it presents. The first sentence is hardly momentous: there are many such purposefully innocuous sentences in *Ulysses*, unobtrusive devices for a momentary thrusting forth of the narrative line. The second sentence, however, stuns with its implication that someone directly in juxtaposition with ourselves knows in advance the extended consequences of an action now in process, regardless of our realization that "Messenger" has no real existence in the text. There are no sentences in *Dubliners* like that nineteenth-century monstrosity, either in terms of its intrusiveness or omniscience.

For the *Dubliners* stories sentences as innocuous as "Messenger took out his matchbox thoughtfully and lit his cigar" are a commonplace, as well as a narrational necessity ("When the Scotch House closed they went round to Mulligan's" – Co 95; "Mr Crofton sat down on a box and looked fixedly at the other bottle on the hob" – Iv 130). Basically concerned with a modicum of forward movement, these statements have no beauty of their own and hardly pretend to any, almost hoping (like Farrington sneaking off to O'Neill's) to pass

8

unnoticed, yet the simple placement of "thoughtfully" and "fixedly" occasionally rescues them from the merely utilitarian. Stephen Dedalus, the creator of a fictional Messenger, is not only engaged in a private exercise of storytelling, but committed to what he knows to be traditionally acceptable as literary presentation, and has doctored reality sufficiently to change a prosaic O'Molloy into a momentous Messenger (a name that translates back into Hebrew as Malachi), and an ordinary cigarette into a prestigious cigar. But "literature" allows for few such simple sentences, and before long it is replaced by the overweighted monstrosity hammered together with six instances of the preposition *that*. The unobtrusive use of the simple past tense (*took out, lit*) gives way to a weightier emphasis on the monumental significance of that past moment (*often thought, looking back, that strange time, the whole aftercourse*), and a first-person narrator not only involves "himself" in the action – in Messenger's act – but implies for himself an omniscience that makes his position as narrator unchallengeable. No such omniscience ever informs the stories of *Dubliners*. Stephen's vignette is an exercise in false narration, a critique through parody of pretentious narrative technique.

"SIGNATURES OF ALL THINGS I AM HERE TO READ"

Many a character in a fictional situation would envy the kind of omniscience with which Messenger's associate is gifted, but few within a "real" situation (as differentiated from a "false lull") are so privileged. The boy who is working his way through some very new experiences in "The Sisters" is making every effort to read the signals that will offer him advance information. His exercise in functional prescience has been in operation for some time, as is apparent from the first sentence of the story, from the moment that Father Flynn was afflicted with a third paralytic attack: "There was no hope for him this time: it was the third stroke" (Si 9). He is wise in attempting to read the future by studying the implications of the present, accepting the transmitted information that a third paralytic seizure means certain death. In phrasing his negative assumptions in terms of "this time", he suggests that the action is completed and that consequently no prognosis is necessary, yet he is quick to indicate that it is death that he is anticipating. The succeeding sentences of "The Sisters" spell out the boy's trust in a sign that will allow him to understand that the future goal has been attained:

Night after night I had passed the house (it was vacation time) and studied the lighted square of window: and night after night I had found it lighted in the same way, faintly and evenly. If he was dead, I thought, I would see the reflection of candles on the darkened blind for I knew that two candles must be set at the head of a corpse. He had often said to me: *I am not long for this world*, and I had thought his words idle. Now I knew they were true. (Si 9)

From these admissions it is obvious that the boy has been living with various signs and portents, from the doubted prophecy of the priest which proved real to the extended assumption of candles which somehow proved false. (The priest's words were doubly prophetic, of the imminent departure from this world and the assumed existence of the next, the latter prophecy a problematic one for the boy throughout his experience with the priest's death.)

Two mysteries exist regarding the boy's short career as an augurer, and neither is solved during the course of the narrative in "The Sisters". At what stage did the information about two candles come into the boy's realm of knowledge, and why did he never see these telltale signs, although he passed the windows "night after night"? The boy seems so positive of his knowledge (*I would see/for I knew*), and also so insistent in his repetitively styled narration that he passed the house every night and yet saw nothing. He may well have passed on the night of the decease and yet not seen a sign that was so manifestly there, for when he goes to visit the corpse and the mourners, he notices that the windows reflect rather than transmit light – the sunset rather than the candles – and that from within he could see that "the candles looked like pale thin flames" in comparison to the prevailing "dusky golden light" (Si 14). These observations are casually transmitted, as if the child who failed to predict the future in missing a given sign had abandoned all interest thereafter in such augury.

Indeed, something vital has definitely gone out of the protagonist. He had undertaken the adventure with such high expectations, not just of being the first to know (or at least to know without having to be told), but actually to *invoke* the mysterious act of Father Flynn's moment of death:

Every night as I gazed up at the window I said softly to myself the word *paralysis*. It had always sounded strangely in my ears. . . .

But now it sounded to me like the name of some maleficent and sinful being. It filled me with fear, and yet I longed to be nearer to it and look upon its deadly work. (Si 9)

That young and presumably innocent child has in fact been wishing for the priest's death, has mumbled his incantation and steeled himself for a horror that he was prepared to enjoy. No casual bystander to the action, he intended to play the part of active catalyst (to assure that our prognostications come true, we will them into existence), and was mysteriously thwarted by the anticipated event taking place without him, in his absence. It is through Old Cotter, a despised surrogate for the all-knowing Father Flynn, that the boy learns of the completed action, and the sentence that begins the informative process is as dull and matter-of-fact as the opening Messenger statement: "Old Cotter was sitting at the fire, smoking, when I came downstairs to supper" (Si 9). Cheated of the immediacy of his longed-for experience, the boy resigns from either allowing himself to react to any further developments or from any further attempt to influence his future. Throughout the visit to the Flynns he remains basically inert and non-communicative.

The power to make things happen is an awesome one, and the boy has over-reached himself in his magical incantations, hoping that by somehow "causing" the priest's death he will not be "caught" by it. To be caught unaware would have meant undergoing an emotional response that he could neither predict nor control; when confronted by Cotter's news he strives to maintain his equilibrium: "I knew that I was under observation so I continued eating as if the news had not interested me" (Si 10). In straining for this pose of indifference, however, he has managed to do for himself what he had failed to do for Father Flynn: through an effort of will he has forced the future to comply with his insistent demand. He returns to the scene of the death, and literally apprehends the "sign" that assures him that the death has indeed occurred, the sign on the door that spells out the details and takes the event out of the hands of Old Cotter. "The reading of the card", he notes, "persuaded me that he was dead and I was disturbed to find myself at check" (Si 12). The self-control that he has achieved seems to him somehow externally imposed, and he continues to look for signs, to read external signatures as he moves away from the house of mourning:

I walked away slowly along the sunny side of the street, reading all the theatrical advertisements in the shop-windows as I went. I found it strange that neither I nor the day seemed in a mourning mood and I felt even annoyed at discovering in myself a sensation of freedom as if I had been freed from something by his death.

(Si 12)

Rather than Father Flynn's death, the boy has somehow caused a death of spirit within himself, although liberated from a relationship with the priest that he did not quite understand, about which he had inexplicably ambivalent feelings. In willing his own condition, controlling his immediate future, he proves oddly vulnerable: the stasis he achieves is disquieting. The ensuing dream seems to him strangely prophetic, yet remains totally uncontrollable, and by the next morning eludes him. To avoid seeing the dead man's face in his night thoughts he "tried to think of Christmas" (Si 11), but invoking December in July has its difficulties. The dream takes possession of him, with the priest as its central figure, yet in the morning he "tried to remember what had happened afterwards in the dream", and realized that he "could not remember the end of the dream" (Si 13–14).

The child's dilemma in "The Sisters" is not just that he is a character in an action that he cannot determine, but that he is also the narrator of a narrative that he cannot control. Limited knowledge and limited experience are the hallmarks of a child's perspective, but despite the presumed convenience of telling the story in the past tense, the narrator shows himself vulnerable at every juncture, since he cannot even for a moment anticipate the next event – or his reaction to it. Cotter catches him unaware; his dream envelopes him against his will and then eludes him; the sunshine disturbs the demands of a proper mood for mourning; and an attempt to take stock of Father Flynn's contributions to his education proves somewhat disconcerting. None the less, he has been making the necessary effort, tracking the events, recording the conversations, and carefully judging his own perceptions. Yet once he comes face to face with the presence of death, and the actual face of the corpse, he loses an important component of his narrational skill. The first jolt is his inability to pray ("I pretended to pray but I could not gather my thoughts because the old woman's mutterings distracted me" – Si 14). The second is more severe: conflicting signals regarding an otherwise simple observation. Still obsessed with accurately reading the signs he encounters, the boy is confronted by the visage of the dead priest:

> The fancy came to me that the old priest was smiling as he lay there in his coffin.
> But no. When we rose and went up to the head of the bed I saw that he was not smiling. (Si 14)

The discrepancies are too overwhelming for the narrator of his own discourse, deprived of comprehending the reality of the smiling priest in his dream, and now dislocated in recording the smile of the priest in what he must assume is wideawake reality. He abstracts himself thereafter as much as he can from his own narrative, allowing himself only the prerogative of moving the furniture of the events ("We blessed ourselves and came away" – Si 14) and disclosing only the most innocuous of his actions ("She pressed me to take some cream crackers also but I declined because I thought I would make too much noise eating them" – Si 15). As mute as the exhausted Nannie, he fades into the role of a total bystander, allowing his aunt and Eliza Flynn to carry on their conversation, independent of his narrational function. During a respite of silence he temporarily comes out of hiding, indicating that "under cover" of silence he tasted his sherry, but soon merges again into the communal silence: "She stopped suddenly as if to listen. I too listened; but there was no sound in the house" (Si 18). Only the most non-commital of individual observations intrude at this ultimate level of stasis in the disembodied narrative ("I knew that the old priest was lying still in his coffin as we had seen him, solemn and truculent in death, an idle chalice on his breast" – Si 18), as he allows Eliza Flynn to sustain the narration along her own lines. The real subject of his intended narration, the reading of the signs of the dead priest's smile, had been disallowed by events he never anticipated and a conflicting narrative he could not comprehend.

In allowing an immature narrator to record his own story (the dominant technique that characterizes all three childhood stories of *Dubliners*), Joyce developed a narrative strategy that constantly calls attention to the limitations of a narrational presence in the act of storytelling. Although there are many indications that the boy in all three cases is intelligent and perhaps even precocious, he is hampered by a pronounced lack of preparation – to encounter reality (usually for the *first* time) and to immediately turn reality into fiction without the self-conscious awareness of an intentional storyteller. At least Messenger's "biographer" has the distinct advantage of a completed script, no matter how disconcerted he is at not having that script in advance, of not having been able to read the signs at the time. By contrast, the boy is handicapped by the necessity for narrational improvisation. Old Cotter and Eliza Flynn, peripheral characters in the lives of the priest and the boy, usurp the narrational prerogative, misplacing the emphasis of the narration by the small dimensions of their perspective. They make few efforts to read the telltale signs, either pronouncing judgements on the basis of inadequate evidence ("I wouldn't like children of mine . . . to have too much to say to a man like that" – Si 10) or passing on the responsibility for evaluation of the evidence to others ("when they saw that, that made them think that there was something gone wrong with him" – Si 18). The boy instinctively knows better, that there is a story to be told and to be told correctly, but is frustrated into silence by the egregious usurpation by others and by his own inexperience.

"SHAKING THE WINGS OF THEIR EXULTANT AND TERRIBLE YOUTH"

The progressive maturation of the boy in the three instances of the childhood tales brings him closer to the realized narrative. Whereas the boy in "The Sisters" is immediately frustrated in his attempt to read the future and determine events of his own life, the narrators in "An Encounter" and "Araby" have made important strides forward in assuming control. To relate the events of a day's miching, unforeseeable events until they actually occur, the protagonist sets the stage with certain past incidents of school life and evening war games. A sense of the past, of action completed and therefore within the storyteller's range of accomplishments, pervades the opening pages. When we are told that "Everyone was incredulous when it was reported that he [Joe Dillon] had a vocation for the priesthood", the narrative stance assumes a certain degree of omniscience, especially with the asserted "Nevertheless it was true" (En 19) that follows immediately after. It is with such assertions that the narrator declares, "I made up mind" (En 21), preparing us for his direct leadership in the carrying out of the day's adventures.

But the ability to shape past occurrences does not carry over into the future, and although the boy is masterful in narrating the confrontation scene in which Father Butler finds Leo Dillon's reading material, he is easily upended during his own confrontation with the queer old josser. In the past incident he can begin by stating that "clumsy Leo Dillon was discovered with a copy of *The Halfpenny Marvel*", and then go on actually to dramatize that discovery with recuperated dialogue ("What have you there in your pocket?" – En 20), in the "present" incident he is unfortunately stymied. Yet he had early on alerted us to his chances of failure ("however well we fought, we never won siege or battle" – En 19), an admission of defeat that does not bode well for a would-be combatant who will eventually insist, "I wanted real adventures to happen to myself" (En 21).

Aware that "real adventures . . . do not happen to people who remain at home: they must be sought abroad" (En 21), the boy decides on a day of adventurous truancy as a dress rehearsal for the real encounter with the reality of experience. He could easily have waited a few weeks (after all, "summer holidays were near at hand" – En 21) and had his day out without skipping classes, but that would have diminished the dangers of such adventures, and deleted the place of "presence" from which to achieve an "absence". With his self-advertisement as a brave pioneer he attempts to determine the shape of the narrative, moulding it to his own advantage, but the naive honesty of an immature prestidigitator reveals more than he intends. Like his predecessor he attempts to read the signs that present themselves before him: at the quays "the barges signalled from far away" and he tries to "decipher the legend" on the Norwegian ship (En 23), the name (legend) that stands for the narrative (legend). In the first case he never indicated that he understands the signals at all (in the window), and in the second he admits that he failed to read the writing (on the stern of the ship). But he persists in examining "the foreign sailors to see had any of them green eyes for I had some confused notion ... " (En 21). Whatever the notion was, it is lost in the narrative lacuna, the place of absence in the ellipsis that eloquently cloaks the completed thought, either because he cannot being himself to disclose the nature of his interest or cannot articulate the substance of his concept, as if only when he found the corroboration of his notion would he comprehend the notion itself.

Looking into their eyes is obviously his method of examination, yet when seated next to the old josser, he assiduously avoids looking at him, sensing a danger that he does not dare confront, as much as he claims to be seeking "real" adventure. Only by inadvertence does he eventually look at the man: "I was surprised at his sentiment and involuntarily glanced up at his face. As I did so I met the gaze of a pair of bottle-green eyes peering at me from under a twitching forehead" (En 27). Avoiding such "reality" from the initial arrival of the man, whose most significant piece of stage business lapses into inexplicable mystery, the narrator abrogates his function by refusing to witness what he does not want to see. "Look what he's doing!" Mahony openly exclaims, but "I neither answered nor raised my eyes" (En 26). Refusing to observe he is unable to report, his sense of positive decision ("I made up my mind to break out of the weariness of school-life for one day at least" – En 21) now disintegrating: "I was still considering whether I would go away or not" (En 26).

As a reliable narrator he served well when the signals were clear and the terrain familiar, as when he looked at the ships along the quay and "saw, or imagined, the geography which had been scantily dosed to me at school gradually taking substance under my eyes" (En 23). This is the stuff that imaginative narratives are made on, but the experienced josser proves to be not only a frightening obstacle to the narration, but a far better magician-storyteller. Divination is his forte from the very beginning, to which the boy proves receptive: as they encounter each other, the boy is chewing "one of those green stems on which girls tell fortunes" and the josser gives the appearance in his slow approach of someone "looking for something in the grass" (En 24). He forecasts the weather ("it would be a very hot summer" – En 25), looks deep into the dark souls of little girls ("all girls were not so good as they seemed to be if one only knew" – En 26), and is a master of sleight-of-hand ("Look what he's doing!" – En 26).

His license to display his tricks is provided him by the protagonist once he has admitted to failure in achieving the stated goal of their adventure: "It was too late and we were too tired to carry out our project of visiting the Pigeon House" (En 24). Not only is the Chapel Perilous never broached, leaving them vulnerable to the monster they never anticipated, but the purpose of the narrative had never been honestly apprehended – not to find adventure, but to prove his own superiority over "a boy named Mahony" (En 21).

The first battle had been too easily won (over "clumsy Dillon", who funked it and forfeited his tanner), but Mahony is deceptively skilful in holding his own, by keeping his eyes open, allowing himself to observe, and usurping the power of *naming* the antagonist. Although unable to solve the mystery of the now named "queer old josser", the narrator can read the signs of his own self-deception ("I was penitent; for in my heart I had always despised him [Mahony] a little" – En 28) and realize the actual thrust of his unconscious motivation.

"ROMANTIC IRELAND'S DEAD AND GONE'

Only in "Araby" is the protagonist the magus of his own narration. External obstacles abound (in the persons of Mrs Mercer and the tipsy uncle, and in delayed trains and inaccessible turnstiles), but he forges ahead relentlessly to find the crux of the narrative, and although he also manages to deceive himself regarding his real motives, he cuts through to a self-revelation that is as honest as it is painful. A seeker and a visionary, he begins with an acknowledged disadvantage: the street he lives on is "blind", and the houses that "gazed at one another with brown imperturbable faces" obviously can see nothing (Ar 29). What he "finds" at first are the detritus of a dead priest ("I found a few paper-covered books"; "I found the late tenant's rusty bicycle-pump" – Ar 29), and although he cannot accurately "read" the significance of the latter sign (his *non sequitur* credits the priest with being charitable in leaving his money to institutions and his furniture to his sister), his interpretation of the former is magical indeed: he likes *The Memoirs of Vidocq* best "because its leaves were yellow" (Ar 29). The narrative quest of "Araby" resides between these approaches, the magically illuminative (or epiphanic) and the inadvertently misleading (the blind street).

As instigator of the narrative the youth in "Araby" conveniently dismisses the past events as incidental to his new life and the story that needs to be told: consequently the frame of his "old life" takes narrative shape as exposition: the world of play, school life, a home with aunt and uncle. A certain sameness identifies that past life once the protagonist realizes the mission he must embark upon ("My aunt was surprised and *hoped* it was not some Freemason affair"; "I watched my master's face pass from amiability to sternness; he *hoped* I was not beginning to idle" – Ar 32; emphasis added). At first he is still part of his peer group, children at play interrupted by the presence of Mangan's older sister ("we watched her from our shadow" – Ar 30), but he soon separates himself from them and regards her now individually as the object of his love: "I stood by the railings looking at her" (Ar 30). The act of love divorces him from the others, and he dedicates himself to worship from afar, alone in the front parlour secretly "watching her door" for her appearance (Ar 30). In various places where she is not present, imagination replaces observation and spying: in the market place "I imagined that I bore my chalice safely through a throng of foes" (AR 31), and "in the classroom her image came between me and the page" (Ar 32).

The narrative that the youth believes he is constructing is a romantic lay, or a *come-all-you* like those he hears in the market-place (Ar 31), a quest story in which he will develop impenetrable vision, see through the thick walls of the castle and find the grail (seeing and finding are his particular skills) to bring back for Mangan's sister. The blind houses on their street have "imperturbable faces", returning no image to the gaze, but like the boy in "The Sisters" looking up at the priest's window or the boy in "An Encounter" looking into the eyes of foreign sailors, he seeks to read mystic signs: "I looked over at the dark house where she lived. I may have stood there for an hour, seeing nothing but the brown-clad figure cast by my imagination" (Ar 33). He is rather adept at intuitive comprehension; when his uncle causes the hallstand to rock, he understands what is happening: "I could interpret these signs", he reports (Ar 33).

What he has failed to see, however, is that in telling the story of Mangan's sister (the narrative of the "other"), he is actually revealing his own inner self, bringing to light his secret motivations. By interpreting the signs in the bazaar, the intensifying darkness, the tawdriness of the surroundings, the paltriness of his funds, and the vulgarity of the overheard conversation, he looks within himself for the first time, all the while assuming that he is looking outward, away from himself. "Gazing up into the darkness", he concludes, "I saw myself as a creature driven and derided by vanity" (Ar 35), an image projected on the dark screen of the bazaar ceiling. The narrative closure leaps ahead of the story presumably being told, completes a story that was being unfolded within the tale that the teller thinks he is pursuing, and his judgement of himself serves as a conclusion to a narrative that he has only now realized has been in progress throughout.

> *Professor MacHugh came from the inner office.*
> *— Talking about the invincibles, he said, did you see that some hawkers were up before the recorder ...*
> *— O yes, J. J. O'Molloy said eagerly. Lady Dudley was walking home through the park to see all the trees that were blown down by that cyclone last year and thought she'd buy a view of Dublin. And it turned out to be a commemoration postcard of Joe Brady or Number One or Skin-the-Goat. Right outside the viceregal lodge, imagine!*
>   (*Ae* 697–704)

What every reader of *Dubliners* is soon aware of is the abrupt transition from the first three stories told in the first-person singular by the central figure to the succeeding twelve stories composed in the third person. The child as innocent narrator of his own material immediately gives way to stories of adults, and the mode of narration shifts as well, as if the Evelines and Marias, the Doyles and Dorans and Duffys cannot be entrusted with their own tales. And these of course are all Dubliners, lifelong residents in a community that prides itself on its gift of the gab and its spellbinding skills in the spinning of a good yarn. Past the awkwardness of childhood, they might each prefer to dictate the terms of their particular narrations, but are prevented from doing so in *Dubliners* by a narrational process that usurps their prerogative. Third-person narration leaves the impression of a tale telling itself, and the degree of objectivity assumed in the narrative stance throughout these twelve tales suggests that no involved participant can anticipate the possibilities of narrative development. Yet many a character locked into the format strives to take over the storytelling function, often with the same frustrations visited on Professor MacHugh. Too many tellers can spoil the tale, and Dubliners are often as impolite as the failed lawyer O'Molloy in stealing the words from each other's mouths.

As with *Ulysses*, where some chapters are heavily laden with dialogue (Aeolus, for example) and others "objectified" (like

Ithaca), the stories in *Dubliners* vary significantly. At first glance it looks as if Eveline Hill has the podium all to herself, and a captive audience as well. The story she would like to tell contrasts the life in Dublin with her father which has become intolerable and the life in Argentina with Frank which will be blissful. She knows the past and hypothesizes the future, attempting to nullify the present. But other voices intrude even in the privacy of her thoughts: Miss Gavan suggests that Eveline might not have been an adequate employee (" – Miss Hill, don't you see these ladies are waiting?" / " – Look lively, Miss Hill, please" – Ev 37); her father asserts that Frank is not to be trusted (" – I know these sailor chaps, he said" – Ev 39); and even her mother "narrates" a story of incomprehensible danger (" – Derevaun Seraun! Derevaun Seraun!" – Ev 40). Each has a separate tale to tell that impinges on and interrupts Eveline's "operettic" version.

"NO VOICE IS WHOLLY LOST"

Within Eveline's rambling apologia, in which idyllic scenes from childhood vie with descriptions of present difficulties, these sharp incisions carry countermanding weight, and she herself underlines the force of her determination to leave by suggesting her own uncertainties. She admits that she can easily be replaced at the Stores, that she is not really in love with Frank, and that her mother's words effect a pull on her that is unrelenting, especially as they reinforce the words on "the coloured print of the promises made to Blessed Margaret Mary Alacoque" (Ev 37). And Frank himself, were he allowed equal time, is indeed a nautical raconteur, but his words have been neutralized by the free indirect style of the narrative and fused through Eveline's personal free associations, so that when we learn that he had "told her stories of the terrible Patagonians" and "had fallen on his feet in Buenos Ayres, he said, and had come over to the old country just for a holiday" (Ev 39), we may also mistrust the inventiveness of the narrative flow and the disquieting placement of that unnecessary source citation ("he said"). When we see him at the moments of closure, Frank is active rather than reflective, and his few words are employed as a magnetic pull on Eveline. Eveline, however, remains mute, frozen in negative decisiveness, aware apparently that the story she had told herself before departure had somehow affected her differently from what she assumed was intended by her own narrative.

The story that Eveline would have liked to construct is embodied in the song "The Lass That Loves a Sailor", and the heroine is a girl named Poppens. Maria's story, which she would not have titled "Clay", is hardly as ambitious and does not project forward into a storybook ending. Maria, in turn, would be content to assume that it has already reached its satisfactory ending in time present. The story would have begun "Once upon a time and a very good time it was" (when Joe and Alphy were loving brothers and Maria was their "proper mother" – Cl 100), and ended when Maria put the kettle on and they all drank tea (for which she was to be crowned a "veritable peace-maker" – Cl 99). In order to tell this childhood fantasy she journeys on All Hallow's Eve to Joe Donnelly's house, but although she brings the spoils of a peaceful victory, she is deflected by more cynical storytellers, not the least of whom are the children who "all said no and looked as if they did not like to eat cakes if they were to be accused of stealing" (Cl 103).

Joe Donnelly insists on retelling the story of Cain and Abel, in which he stars as the good brother who none the less has survived, as well as a complementary tale in which he symbolically overthrows the father figure ("repeating for her a smart answer which he had made to the manager" – Cl 104). It is also apparent that Mrs Donnelly has a readymade one about an old woman who lives out her remaining life in a convent and is therefore no burden to anyone, but Joe eventually realizes that the story that is unfolding before his eyes is of a wasted life soon to be extinguished, and in order to cover his unease and embarrassing prescience he offers his Tale of a Corkscrew.

Divination is invariably a narrative with only a fixed number of closures, but an open range of possibilities. In Maria's case a malicious narrator, in keeping with the nature of the ghostly holiday, has tampered with the script, determining Maria's future with the substitution of a lump of common garden clay. Mrs Donnelly, however, acts quickly to change the scenario and is probably herself as responsible for the prayerbook resolution as the girls from next door were for the clay resolution. Other Dubliners also indulge in attempts to read the future, Jimmy Doyle employing a deck of cards to learn about his own. The story that was supposed to end with his profitable investment in an automobile enterprise had begun with his father's straightforward attainment of financial success as a merchant prince of butchers, the traditional bourgeois success story. There was, however, a disconcerting "loop" in the paternal narrative, the political selling-out that resulted in police contracts, and Jimmy attempts to straighten the loop, to "influence" the narrative by making his own nationalist speech in the face of the opposing Englishman, sealing his fate in the delicately balanced card game. And in the committee room a handful of political canvassers peer into the dim firelight in hope of predicting (determining) their future.

What the canvassers hope to find out is whether Tierney will be forthcoming with their pay, but they are easily deflected into wondering whether he will (instead) send over a dozen bottles of stout. Both are within the realm of fictional possibility, but no story of this mood and tone can be expected to have a double happy ending, and between possibility (immediate payment) and probability (the sop of a dozen of stout), the futureless denizens of the committee room blandly accept the false resolution. Their collective existences (each has his own individual story to tell of economic hardship) have brought them to static acceptance, and no one can offer anything resembling satisfactory closure, although the "possibilities" are implied: the return of Parnell, a return to Parnell's ideals, a scheme that will prevent the visit of Edward VII, a dump-Tierney political campaign that will succeed, secure employment for each of the canvassers. Tierney, after all, has written the script, manipulating each of his ineffectual characters without himself having to participate, and as happens so frequently toward the end of each of the *Dubliners* stories, Joyce forecloses prematurely, hinting at narratives unrealized within the existing texts.

"WHO CAN SPEAK FOR THE DUMB?"

Even in a society where speech is golden there are the inarticulate with their own tales to tell, but little or no capacity in the telling. Women especially are disadvantaged in the masculine world of witty repartee and cutting responses, so that both Eveline and Maria lack both a receptive audience and a narrational skill, the former attempting to write her story in letters left behind, to her brother and to her father. Maria is particularly tongue-tied, invariably having the story taken away from her by more aggressive speakers: the Matron and Ginger Mooney write their narrative of Maria as guardian of the peace (fairy tale); Joe of Maria as symbol of motherhood (sentimental saga); Lizzie Fleming and the salesgirl in the cake shop of Maria as prospective bride (ironic comedy). Maria keeps her version secret in the face of such distortion and derision, what she experiences as confusing deflection, contemplating with "quaint affection" her "nice tidy little body" (Cl 101). Only when pressed into performance does she reveal in fictional disguise the narrative that she had so often rehearsed, and her singing of "I Dreamt that I Dwelt", like Aunt Julia's rendition of "Arrayed for the Bridal", allows her to make her narrational confession. That she defaults after the first verse, unable to continue on toward real completion, attests once again to the pathos of her untold tale and unlived life.

Occasionally, a Dublin woman, finding her way barred to the exposition of her own discourse, bides her time for two decades before finding an alternative means of self-expression. Mrs. Kearney, having necessarily suppressed the story of ivory manners by filling her mouth with Turkish delight, eventually transfers her attention to writing the success story of her musically talented daughter. With decanters of whisky, and blush-pink charmeuse, and offers of two-shilling tickets, she has bought herself an audience who would presumably sense that behind the thin veneer of Kathleen's artistry (she is after all only an accompanist) looms the saga of a mother's mastery, the tale of a Miss Devlin who had to bury her light under a bushel for so many years. But Holohan, Fitzpatrick and the anonymous committee prove as insensitive to self-sacrifice and dedication as the suitors had been to her ivory manners, singing their own song of making music pay in philistine Dublin. Their official spokesman, who will broadcast their message in print to the public, is O'Madden Burke, surrogate journalist pressed into service, and he has the curtain line in "A Mother": " – You did the proper thing, Holohan, said Mr O'Madden Burke, poised upon his umbrella in approval" (Mo 149). His is the surface version that governs the printed narrative in *Dubliners*, an indictment of a frustrated woman (the closing "moral" is that she is not a "proper mother") who ruins her daughter's career through an incomprehensible obstinacy.

The narrative of feminine consciousness surfaces at several instances in *Dubliners*. We suspect that Mrs Kernan in "Grace" has a tale to tell of a vain paycock of a husband, of bringing up children in a household in which too much of the paycheck goes into silk hats and gaiters and numerous drinks, or of singlehandedly keeping the Faith in the face of her husband's backsliding. But she has long since learned to hold her tongue, resigned but not defeated ("for twenty-five years she had kept house shrewdly for her husband" – Gr 156), and now that he has bitten off a piece of his tongue and been rendered incommunicative, she could conceivably take advantage of the pause to narrate in her own voice. Yet she chooses to do so only in the privacy of her own thoughts: "She was tempted to see a curious appropriateness in his accident and, but that she did not wish to seem bloody-minded, she would have told the gentlemen that Mr Kernan's tongue would not suffer by being shortened" – Gr 157–8). Instead, she hands over all story-telling responsibilities to the men: "I leave it all in your hands, Mr Cunningham" (Gr 157). And the men in "Grace" are not shy in holding forth at great length.

With Kernan incapacitated, gabbers galore descend upon him. The official trio have rehearsed a fairytale of religious redemption, although several layers of narrative are operative within each of them, and allowed to talk along his own lines any one of them would veer off into an individually structured tale. The stories that they prefer to suppress, however, filter to the surface despite their intentions: that of "an unpresentable woman who was an incurable drunkard" (Cunningham's Tale – Gr 157), of "inexplicable debts" (Power's Tale – Gr 154), of a "line of life" that "had not been the shortest distance between two points" (M'Coy's Tale – Gr 158), and, when he accidentally becomes part of the group, that of "a modest grocer" who "had failed in business" (Fogarty's Tale – Gr 166). On their way to their particular Canterbury (the Gardiner Street church), these pilgrims weave tales instead that deflect away from their unstated prologues: the 70-year-old epileptic whose bitten tongue grew back, the "ignorant bostooms" in the police force (Gr 160), the history of the Jesuits (expurgated), the history of the Papacy (transaccidentated), and so forth. Each is a disguised narrative whose function is to distract temporarily from the direct thrust of the intended text, the Redemption of the Fallen Kernan.

Although Martin Cunningham has the respect of his hearers and the necessary skill in weaving a good yarn (in *Ulysses* he takes away the Reuben J. Dodd anecdote from Bloom when he senses that it will be marred in the telling), in the Kernan sickroom he finds himself in a false position of having to relate a story that everyone had already heard, the punch line having already been disclosed, "65, catch your cabbage" (Gr 161). He tries to make the best of a bad situation, but it is apparent that the false context of the narrative works against him, that the delaying tactic (like that of the Belvedere College director in *A Portrait* babbling about "jupes") reveals its artificial condition, the warp in the weave. All elliptical narratives in "Grace" lead to the efficacy of the concluding "Parson's Tale", Father Purdon's parable-sermon on the Children of This World, which he admits can undergo pragmatic blue-pencilling at will, an adaptable cautionary tale: "I find this wrong and this wrong. But, with God's grace, I will rectify this and this" (Gr 174).

The women of "The Dead", as if to countermand the vow of silence foisted on them, mount a major narrative campaign, especially in the. light of masculine inadequacy. Freddy Malins is so drunkenly hilarious that he cannot bring his anecdote to a satisfactory completion, "repeating words of his last phrase as well as his fit of laughter would allow him" (De 185). Mr Browne offends his genteel listeners with his vulgar quip, "so that the young ladies, with one instinct, received his speech in silence" (De 183). And Gabriel Conroy worries over the aptness of his quotations for his after-dinner speech, the target of his pointed remark having already eluded him by leaving before dinner. As deficient as are Aunt Julia's "Arrayed for the Bridal" and Mary Jane's "Academy piece, full of runs and difficult passages" (De 186), and as impolitic as is Aunt Kate's diatribe against the exclusion of women from church choirs (denying women their voices), other women at the Morkans' party are far more successful in their narrative thrusts. Lily scores exceptionally well against Gabriel with her tale of misprized love ("The men that is now is only all palaver and what they can get out of you" – De 178). Unaffected by the necessities of bourgeois demeanour, the caretaker's daughter is aware of the relationship between narrational colouring and ulterior intentions, and would have seen through the Cunningham–Power–M'Coy camouflage. Molly Ivors, on the other hand, freed by her political ideology from bourgeois pretensions, follows through with her case against the West Briton, a "frank-mannered talkative young lady" (De 187) effectively stating her case for the West of Ireland. (Even Mrs Malins's "tongue rambled on" (De 190) far more smoothly than her son's.)

FAILED NARRATIVES

Gabriel is at cross-purposes with himself, and there are three possible storylines that he eventually pursues. His speech serves as his *apologia pro vita sua* despite his original intentions, as he identifies with the reigning spirit of Irish hospitality, but it is also apparent that he has become the ordained chronicler of the past. He is openly identified as "G.C.", the book reviewer, a transmitter of stories already published, participating in the process of twice-told tales, and it is in that capacity that he launches his final thrust at emissaries of the past, the "late lamented Patrick Morkan, our grandfather" and "a horse by the name of Johnny" (De 207). Yet Gabriel succeeds only in titillating Mr Browne, in effect "giving scandal to Mr Browne who is of the other persuasion" (De 194), much to the embarrassment of his aunts. While he is engaged in this twice-told tale (everyone has heard it before except Browne), Gabriel is unaware that a far more important narrative is being presented upstairs.

Although Bartell D'Arcy may be a flawed narrator with a hoarse throat, he manages to weave a musical yarn of the Irish past, of Miss Ivor's West of Ireland, one that reawakens in Gretta an ancient narrative of her own. Not only is she enthralled by D'Arcy's presentation of "The Lass of Aughrim", but realizes herself to be an active participant in the ballad, eventually taking it on as her own. Gabriel had secretly been rehearsing a love story, unconsciously instigated by his viewing of a "picture of the balcony scene in *Romeo and Juliet*" (De 186), and perhaps encouraged by his gazing at the phallic Wellington Monument outside the window. His is to be a story of requited love, once told in the past when he and Gretta were a newly married couple, and now to be re-enacted in the Gresham Hotel. But it is Gretta as the Lass of Aughrim who prevails at the Gresham as the raconteur, abetted inadvertently by Gabriel's series of leading questions. Gabriel becomes so enmeshed in Gretta's narrative of star-crossed lovers that he has lost his own drift, surrendered his role as tribal *seanachie*, and yielded to the more spellbinding account, his own love-story stillborn within him, a failed narrative tentatively titled *Distant Music*. Gretta Conroy's "unheard" music is sweeter.

Dubliners is shot through with such failed narratives, one of the most potent that of the heavy-tongued Farrington. His would be a simple story to tell, of his spectacular triumph over the villainous

Mr Alleyne, and although he primes himself with a slightly titivated version and sufficient cash reserves to establish his base as teller, he finds the tale taken out of his mouth by an experienced usurper, Higgins: "The men asked him to give his version of it, and he did so with great vivacity" (Co 93). (Farrington just does not have the credentials or credibility, not so much mistrusted as an unreliable narrator as an unimaginative one, not capable of the best "version".) A more pathetic failure, however, is that of Bob Doran, who finds himself with no story to tell since he cannot honestly present an account of his wooing and winning of Polly Mooney without thoroughly discrediting himself. He realizes that he is at the centre of a narrative that he can neither control nor gainsay: "All the lodgers in the house knew something of the affair; details had been invented by some" (Bo 65); he has already committed it to his confessor, and "the priest had drawn out every ridiculous detail of the affair" (Bo 65). Nor can he face his ideal auditor, the one who would take an inordinate interest in the events ("The affair would be sure to be talked of and his employer would be certain to hear of it" – Bo 65–6). Doran is saddled with a story that may not be told, but one which others are already relating as gossip, and of the three people from whom it should be kept secret, one has already heard it from him (his Father Confessor) and another is slated to as well (Polly's mother).

One of the most adept talkers, reputed for "his adroitness and eloquence" (Tw 50), is the Lenehan of "Two Gallants", who none the less confronts an inner narrative that he does not dare articulate: the story of a contented citizen, with "a warm fire to sit by and a good dinner to sit down to", one who would "be able to settle down in some snug corner and live happily" (Tw 58). But he has abrogated any rights to such a personal narrative, and although his "tongue was tired for he had been talking all afternoon in a public-house", he is doomed to babble on and wander on, repeating his "vast stock of stories, limericks and riddles" (Tw 50) in lieu of the compelling narrative that occasionally surfaces in his mind and demands to be told. Lenehan is as much the victim of his narrational skills as he is of an inability to confront an inner compulsion for which no outlet exists.

Few characters in *Dubliners* are as verbal as Lenehan, yet the oral storyteller requires an audience willing to listen (either without interrupting or with the knack of encouraging the speaker), but Lenehan spends most of the evening alone, prey to visions – "In his imagination he beheld the pair of lovers walking along some dark road" (Tw 57) – and the nagging alternative scene of his imaginary hearth. Detached from that "public-house in Dorset Street" (Tw 50), he is deprived of the social ambience for his stories, limericks and riddles, a counterpart of the Jimmy Doyle who in the racing car shouting into the wind exemplifies the same deprivation within a presumable social sphere. Farrington's parade of pubs (Davy Byrne's, the Scotch House, John Mulligan's) should have been ideal arenas for his recitation, yet they actually militated against him and favoured better talkers and stronger wrestlers.

The literary storyteller, on the other hand, thrives on the disadvantages of loneliness and privacy, and yet Gabriel Conroy for one discovers himself in a complex social situation all evening, one in which he has constantly to converse, contend and contradict, to talk himself out of a series of difficulties for which he was unprepared. Thomas Chandler walks even more eagerly into a social trap, also unaware just how unprepared he is to translate his "literary" talents into social discourse. In his own arena, walking alone across the bridge over the Liffey, he has a chance to create a personal narrative about "poor stunted houses" as "a band of tramps, huddled together along the river-banks, their old coats covered with dust and soot, stupefied by the panorama of sunset and waiting for the first chill of night to bid them arise, shake themselves and begone" (Li 73). Nowhere else in *Dubliners* does a better imaginary possibility emerge for a coherent narrative outside the frame of the stories themselves, yet it is immediately apparent that Little Chandler will never give fictive life to his band of tramps. The narrative that he fabricates instead concerns a T. Malone Chandler, poet of "the Celtic school" (Li 74), a central character destined to evaporate upon contact with the hard-featured reality of Ignatius Gallaher.

Gallaher has taken up his stance at the bar – his narrative stance – and all that Chandler ever succeeds in doing is to provide grist for Gallaher's narrational mill, recounting the story of foreign travel, sinful cities and wicked duchesses. In the face of such tall tales Little Chandler seems quite willing to efface himself in order to imagine himself as Ignatius Gallaher. As Gallaher of "the London Press" (Li 72) he prefers to forget that he has had his exile forced upon him, and Chandler, who had earlier been quite adept at writing that sordid tale, temporarily forgets as well. By teasing the stay-at-home of "old jogalong Dublin" (Li 78) he undermines the

fictive centre of Chandler's vision of the houses along the river-
banks, relegating him instead to one of the tramps. Like the dog
viewing himself in the pond, Chandler drops his bone in envy of
Gallaher's, preferring the exotic narrative not of his own experience, but it does not take him long to react against Gallaher's "false
lull" and attempt to recover lost ground in the pursuit of his own
narrative line. Of the two characters created by Little Chandler in
anticipation of the prodigal's return, that of the disgraced fugitive
and that of the London *bon vivant*, the appearance of the *bon vivant*
reawakens vestiges of the exile who had departed when he "got
mixed up in some shady affair" (Li 72).

Once Chandler has retreated home and is reading Byron aloud,
he establishes a narrational base for an encounter between Thomas
Chandler and Lord Byron, a story of a literary relationship superior
to any imagined with Gallaher. His captive audience, however, is
his discomfited child, whose cries destroy the delicate beginnings
of the new fiction. Despite all his inspirations, T. Malone Chandler
has written nothing down on paper, not the saga of the Liffey
houses, or of the Great Gallaher of the London Press, or of Lord
Byron passing on his baton to the poet of the Celtic School. Even
Joe Hynes has committed himself in writing, to a tale of the lone
disciple, the Last of the Parnellites, keeping alive the ideals of
Charles Stewart Parnell and winning the turncoats back to the true
path. It is unfortunate for Hynes that the Orangeman Crofton
should be in the audience to vitiate the narrative by dubbing it "a
very fine piece of writing" (Iv 135).

James Duffy also attempts to write the book of himself, shunning
both a readership and outside participants in his narcissistic text.
His work is entitled *Bile Beans*, a personal epic in epigrams, the
central character of which lives "at a little distance from his body"
(Pa 108), and its unifying theme is that "every bond . . . is a bond to
sorrow" (Pa 112). *Bile Beans* is an exercise in the literature of stasis:
the hero lives every day like every other, with "neither companions
nor friends, church or creed. . . . without any communion with
others" (Pa 109). It is a tale assured of its immortality since without
change it cannot suffer deterioration. By tightly enclosing the
parameters of the narrative, by eliminating all possibilities and
restricting it exclusively to the probable, the text is airtight and
fixed. Nor does the relationship with Mrs Sinico violate its fixity,
protected as it is by Duffy's antiseptic fictions regarding that
relationship: he allows Captain Sinico the fiction (highly improb-

able) that "his daughter's hand was in question" (Pa 110), and on Mrs Sinico he foists the fiction (quite impossible) of his ascending "to an angelical stature" (Pa 111). Living at a distance from his body he can keep that distance from hers: "he heard the strange impersonal voice which he recognized as his own, insisting on the soul's incurable loneliness" (Pa 111). She, however, was involved in creating her own (kinetic) version of their relationship, and when she frightens and offends him by the passion of that singular interpretation, Duffy writes her out of his narrative. It remains only for a Tolstoi to write her into an *Anna Karenina*.

Yet the narrative that dominates "A Painful Case" is a newspaper report that lends the story its title, the two narratives masking each other. For Duffy the suggestion that he "write out his thoughts" is repulsive: "To compete with phrasemongers" and "submit himself to the criticisms of an obtuse middle class" (Pa 111). Devoid of an active and developing narrative of his own, Duffy finds his static version impotent against the rendition presented by journalistic phrasemongers. He had refused to acknowledge Mrs Sinico's role in his narrative and shunned collaboration with her on hers. He is therefore forced to suffer the newspaper account of her life and death, a narrative that leaves him out entirely, and by so doing calls into question his actual existence. In a context in which a "Mr H. B. Patterson Finlay" (Pa 114) can hold forth at length, Mr James Duffy has no tale to tell. Although he is one of the most literate and literary of Dubliners, he is trapped in a paralytic enclosure, only willing to read the book of himself when it is too late and there are no pages left to turn.

Mr. Duffy's predicament is diagnostic of the frustrated, untold tales that the Joycean narrative none the less tells in *Dubliners*, in sharp contradistinction to the constant packaging of personal narratives that are the property and hallmark of Stephen Dedalus in *A Portrait of the Artist as a Young Man*. When the contiguous and overlapping worlds of the Dubliners and the Dedaluses coalesce in *Ulysses* (a text that still has its validity as the sixteenth story of *Dubliners*), the Duffy legacy of a writer-who-does-not-write divides itself in various ways between Stephen Dedalus and Leopold Bloom, the former successful only in producing a poetic quatrain in which *other tellers* seem to have had a hand already, and the latter a middle-aged artist of only lagging pretension and imagined intentions. Stephen, of course, has managed to talk away a Shakespeare theory and a newly plotted parable in the course of a few hours, replicating his father's oral feats but hardly fulfilling his vocation during a day generally left free for writing, while Bloom, especially in Hades, reveals no great gift of the gab and hypothesizes small narratives in his thoughts to rival the literary output of one Philip Beaufoy. None of them, tentative as they are, has the consistency, incisiveness and structure of the hypothetical visit to the Gouldings that Stephen frames in his mind, yet there is no clue as to whether Stephen realizes the literary potential of the Strasburg Terrace vignette or that he will ever set it down on library slips. And Molly Bloom contains within her thoughts dozens of potential narratives – but thereby hangs *another* tale.

2

Narrative Gnomonics:
The Spectres in the Tales

> – *What is a ghost? Stephen said with tingling energy. One who has faded into impalpability through death, through absence, through change of manners.*
>
> SC 147–9

In Tom Stoppard's *Rosencrantz and Guildenstern Are Dead*, as he is about to disappear off stage Rosencrantz says, "Now you see me, now you ... " – the last word, like the character himself, lost in the closing ellipsis. Readers know from Shakespeare's text that he is now a ghost through death; auditors know from Stoppard's play that he is a ghost through absence. The pregnant ellipsis is itself a ghost through absence, suspended aloft and rattling its chains, unspoken but nevertheless "heard" by the process of subliminal anticipation, as we instinctively complete the familiar line by resorting to a pre-existing text. The gnomon of Euclid resurfaces thousands of years later in the opening paragraph of "The Sisters", trailing clouds of meaning after itself, perhaps undreamed of in Euclid's philosophy, probably only dimly perceptible to the young dilettante of words who is the central intelligence of the story, and variously apprehended by the variety of readers of *Dubliners*.

Gnomon co-exists in the boy's mind in an unholy trinity with paralysis and simony, newly learned, unclearly understood, and yet endowed with elements of linguistic magic. Paralysis is the *new* word that he incarnates as "some maleficent and sinful being" (Si 9) come to claim the dead priest, and therefore not necessarily differentiated from the priest himself, a malevolent apparition. By extension, simony (actually derived from the name of a personified Simon Magus) is assumed to be one who sometimes appears but should be kept away, another sinful being that is the sin itself. Gnomon, on the other hand, although directly associated with its "author", seems much more abstract, mathematical and remote, a non-appearance suggesting a presence made palpable only by the concept of its absence. In "Araby", books (the "ghosts" of their authors) replace words in a more sophisticated unholy trinity: "*The Abbot*, by Walter Scott, *The Devout Communicant* and *The Memoirs of Vidocq*" (Ar 29). One of them has lost its author, and another has absorbed the author into the title, a ghost by implication, while still another sets up the disparity between the figure in the title and the author himself, a ghost by change of manners.

"MY FAMILIAR, AFTER ME, CALLING . . . "

The ghosts who haunt *Dubliners* outnumber those conjured up either by William Shakespeare or Henrik Ibsen or Charles Dickens, beginning with Father Flynn himself and followed by green-eyed sailors, Father Butler, O'Donovan Rossa, Ernest Hill, Mrs Farrington, Alphy Donnelly, Mrs Sinico, Charles Stewart Parnell, Richard J. Tierney, Johannes Josef Ignatz von Dollinger, Father Constantine Conroy, Michael Furey, Patrick Morkan and his horse Johnny, and hosts of others, including the Holy Ghost. Not all are necessarily dead, although all are significantly absent or – better still – metamorphosed.

In a collection of stories that begins with the demise of Father Flynn, anticipated in his absence, apprehended in his death and eventually realized in his change of manners, the priestly presence is most often superseded by the priestly absence. Flynn is dead before the boy is aware that he has actually died, and when apprised of the news by Cotter feigns indifference rather than give the adults the satisfaction of seeing his reaction, "denying" the death. Later he finds that the pretence of indifference has evolved into a sustained absence of emotional response, and the card on the door that is the death notice acknowledges that even before his death the priest was a ghost by absence ("formerly of S. Catherine's Church, Meath Street" – Si 12). Even before an official verification of the death, the boy is afraid of being haunted: "In the dark of my room I imagined that I saw again the heavy grey face of the paralytic" (Si 11). The ghost is exorcized from his conscious thoughts, only to materialize in his dream, strangely smiling, the smile reflected in the boy's responsive smile, until roles are reversed and the child absolves the priest of simony: "I felt that I too was smiling feebly as if to absolve the simoniac of his sin" (Si 11). The smile recurs when the boy views the corpse, but it is only the ghost of a smile, first a product of the boy's "fancy" that he was smiling, then the death of that "ghost": "he was not smiling" (Si 14).

Each of the three childhood stories has its obligatory Catholic cleric, but whereas Father Flynn is so recently deceased the priest that haunts the dead-ended house in "Araby" is remote, displaced, anonymous and unrelated to the boy who now tenants his transferred residence. His ghostly domain is the "waste room behind the kitchen" that is "littered with old useless papers" (Ar 29); his legacy is a trio of abandoned books reflecting either his interests (ostensible or covert) or rejection (purposeful discardings) – in either case they transfer to the accidental recipient who prefers the one with the yellow pages. Bracketed by these dead priests, Father Butler of "An Encounter" is very much alive, but his presence is confined to his school so that the truants in absenting themselves from classes for the day manage to disengage themselves from his living presence. None the less, the spectre of Father Butler threatens to hover over at least one of them as they plan their disengagement. A shadow of the brother who was already destined for the priesthood, Leo Dillon endows the priest with extraterritorial powers. He expresses himself as "afraid that we might meet Father Butler or someone out of the college" (En 21) – Leo is not yet schooled in the Dedalus dictum that "We walk through ourselves, meeting robbers, ghosts, giants, old men, young men, wives, widows, brothers-in-love, but always meeting ourselves" (SC 1044–6). Nor is he as sanguine about it as Leopold Bloom: "Might meet a robber or two. Well, meet him" (Ca 91–2).

For Leo it is a fear that no rational disclaimer can dispel, and he voluntarily becomes a ghost through absence, preferring to face the priest in the flesh than risk the priest in spirit at the Pigeon House. He silently opts for becoming a truant from the planned truancy. By contrast the insensitive Mahony, whom the protagonist-narrator has already distanced himself from by calling him "a boy named Mahony", provides what the protagonist considers a "sensible" rejoinder ("Mahony asked, very sensibly, what would Father Butler be doing out at the Pigeon House" – En 21), the answer to which would be obvious to anyone who believes in ghosts. Lulled by this logic, the protagonist risks ghostly encounters on the day's adventures, but he and Mahony manage to procrastinate sufficiently in their meanderings toward their destination so as never actually to arrive at the Pigeon House, it too an unrealized goal that may portend more than it promises. In effect, Father Butler's spirit may well be in residence there and holding the territory unchallenged.

In the adult stories of *Dubliners* a notable absence of priests becomes endemic, in sharp contradistinction to the pivotal roles they play in childhood. The absence/anonymity established in "Araby" has its counterpart in "Eveline", the link story that connects childhood with the adult world, once again associating priestly non-presence with pages turning yellow:

> And yet during all those years she had never found out the name of the priest whose yellowing photograph hung on the wall above the broken harmonium beside the coloured print of the promises made to Blessed Margaret Mary Alacoque. He had been a school friend of her father. Whenever he showed the photograph to a visitor her father used to pass it with a casual word:
> – He is in Melbourne now. (Ev 37)

The tone of indirection, the degree of insignificance, the remoteness of the Australian location, the indifference in Eveline's idle curiosity – all these relegate the departed cleric to obscurity. And there is no one until "Ivy Day in the Committee Room" to represent the Dublin clergy in *Dubliners*.

As a prelude to the mysterious appearance of Father Keon in "Ivy Day", there is the casual mention of "Father Burke's name" (Iv 123), conscripted into service by candidate Tierney's canvassers as one of the nominators of their man, a ghostly backer, his name having ironic reverberations once the revered Father Tom Burke is eulogized in "Grace". (At the other end of the onomastic spectrum is Daniel Burke, the Dublin publican in whose premises James Duffy has his lunch – Tierney is also a publican.) It is Father Keon, of course, who excites the interests of the canvassers, an apparition out of nowhere, the uninvited guest, bundled up so that his clerical collar is concealed, hovering in the doorway of the darkened committee room, seeking someone who is not there. (His face has "the appearance of damp yellow cheese" – Iv 125.) First designated as a "person resembling a poor clergyman or a poor actor" (Iv 125), Keon is immediately classified in terms of a false façade (a clergyman dissembling? an actor impersonating?), and Henchy, solicitously attempting to establish identity, manages to voice a disbelief in his very existence: "O, Father Keon! . . . Is that you?" (Iv 126). Failing to find the object of his visit, the priest quickly and self-effacingly disappears, leaving behind enthralled speculation:

What is he exactly? . . .
Is he a priest at all? . . .
And how does he knock it out? . . .
Is he attached to any chapel or church of institution or –

(Iv 126–7)

The lapsed question, although answered in the negative, resurfaces immediately in a new context emphasizing once again that which is missing from the committee room, that which their missing employer could easily have provided from his own premises: "Is there any chance of a drink itself?" (Iv 127). Despite the temporary fascination with the "black sheep" pastor, he is summarily allowed to fade into inconsequence, replaced by a dozen of stout.

Father Keon has the almost unique distinction of being a ghost through *change of manners*, although he may have an analogue in the famous Father Purdon of "Grace", as obvious and visible a cleric as Keon is devious and invisible. "Grace" is the particular story in *Dubliners* in which the clergy are of pronounced importance, although the centrality of religion does not guarantee the sanctity of ecclesiastical stature. As the comforters gather around the Kernan sickbed, at which Fogarty intrudes as the uninvited, unexpected guest, the talk is of popes who do not behave like popes ("there were some bad lots", Cunningham concedes – Gr 168), but write poems on photography; cardinals who either change their beliefs or leave the church; priesthoods that are "unworthy of the name" (Gr 164); the Jesuit order that "never fell away" (Gr 164), although its having been suspended on several occasions never is acknowledged by those assembled in the sickroom; and a sermon that is "not exactly a sermon, you know. It's just a kind of a friendly talk, you know" (Gr 165). Mrs Kernan's contribution to Catholic orthodoxy introduces the banshee as part of a quadrilateral Trinity, paralleling Fogarty's presence as a Fourth Comforter.

When Father Purdon does make his appearance, he justifies his reputation as "a man of the world like ourselves" (Gr 164), although Kernan has never heard of him, and he lectures on double-entry spiritual accountancy. It is a resuscitated Kernan who attends the retreat, apparently unmindful that no spiritual comforter from the Church had been present at his bedside, only well-meaning but ill-informed laity involved in luring him through duplicity to the Gardiner Street church. In "The Dead", no spiritual emanation attends the Christmas-time festivities at the Morkans' either, although the reigning pope is taken to task for eliminating women from the choirs, and monks at Mount Melleray are lauded for sleeping in their coffins, although not yet dead. Particularly conspicuous for his absence is Gabriel's brother, Father Constantine Conroy, senior curate at Balbriggan. No one mentions him at all during the course of the evening, and it is only in a photograph that Constantine is present, seen only by this brother, not as a priest but as a child "dressed in a man-o'-war suit" (De 186).

"DEATH HAS LOST ITS DOMINION"

When Gabriel Conroy posits a general paralytic condition of snow falling generally throughout Ireland, he envisions an Oughterard graveyard as a paradigm of Ireland, "snow falling . . . upon all the living and the dead" (De 224). These two discrete categories had undergone a series of fusions in "The Dead", a process anticipated by almost every story in *Dubliners*. Deaths occur only in "The Sisters" and "A Painful Case", but the margin separating life and death is often depleted: Eveline Hill is not yet twenty, yet had lost a mother and brother; even a childhood playmate, Tizzie Dunn, is already dead. She herself has undergone a change from childhood into a prematurely responsibility-ridden young adult, for whom the efficacy of escape is justified by the changes in the world around her ("Everything changes" – Ev 37). When she assumes that "Now she was going to go away like the others", does she mean like the Waters, who "had gone back to England" (Ev 37), or like Tizzie Dunn? The photograph of the forgotten priest returns her own image should she leave; she may not be able to imagine her prospective house in Buenos Ayres, but she can visualize herself *absent* from her own home, a fading, yellowing, discarded memory, a vacuum that only the dust fills. The fear of non-existence eventually paralyses Eveline into remaining a ghost in her own home.

The motif of negative haunting – the absence of an expected ghost – is introduced in the opening story as the child realizes his

lack of emotional response to the news of the priest's death, and
has its fuller development in "A Painful Case". By maintaining no
real contact with other living beings, Duffy has insulated himself
from their ghostly visitations after death ("He lived his spiritual life
without any communion with others, visiting his relatives at
Christmas and escorting them to the cemetery when they died" –
Pa 109). By living "at a little distance from his body, regarding his
own acts with doubtful side-glances" (Pa 108), he has established
himself as his own ghost, a comfortable ghost he knows and has
accommodated himself to. Although the official verdict records that
"No blame attached to anyone" (Pa 115), Duffy suspects that he has
compromised himself into qualifying as Mrs Sinico's intended
victim by the inadvisable relationship he had temporarily conducted with her. (Captain Sinico, a ghost through absence, had
created a vacuum into which Duffy allowed himself to be drawn.)

As long as Duffy can convince himself that Mrs Sinico herself
was to blame, he can remain free of her haunting. As soon as he
implicates himself as responsible for her neglect (he too a ghost
through absence), the danger of her ghost accosting him becomes
imminent: "She seemed to be near him in the darkness. At moments he seemed to feel her voice touch his ear, her hand touch his.
He stood still to listen. Why had he withheld life from her? Why
had he sentenced her to death? He felt his moral nature falling to
pieces" (Pa 117). A third turn of the screw, however, eliminates any
possibility of ectoplasmic contact from the dead Mrs Sinico. Instead, it is the *absence* of any such emanation that haunts Mr Duffy:

> He could not feel her near him in the darkness nor her voice
> touch his ear. He waited for some minutes listening. He could
> hear nothing: the night was perfectly silent. He listened again:
> perfectly silent. He felt that he was alone.
>
> (Pa 117)

The ease with which the dead evaporate from memory is a
subject that is of some concern to Leopold Bloom ("People talk
about you a bit: forget you. . . . Even Parnell. Ivy day dying out" –
Ha 853–5), almost as if he had witnessed the events a year or so
earlier in the Tierney committee room. Parnell's ghost, wanly
evoked by Joe Hynes, fails to generate fire or warmth among the
jejune political canvassers; nor does the ethereal presence of Christ
fare much better in the hothouse atmosphere of the Morkans'

Christmas party, where no bursting forth of an epiphany illumines the twelfth night of the Yule season. Father Flynn's corpse is as devoid of spirit as his dropped chalice had been of sacramental wine; Eveline Hill's mother is recalled for her dying gibberish; and the missing mother of the Donnelly brothers had long since been replaced by Maria: even while alive she had been relegated to a back seat ("Mamma is mamma but Maria is my proper mother" – Cl 100) and then displaced completely, her death presumably responsible for the "break-up at home" (Cl 100).

In "The Dead" the dead outnumber the living, literally as well as metamorphically. The presence of Gabriel, the two aunts and niece Mary Jane is overbalanced by the absence of the third sister Ellen, Gabriel's mother; of the brother Pat, Mary Jane's father; of Gabriel's father, T. J. Conroy; of grandfather Patrick Morkan; and of Mary Jane's mother – by implication, although she is never mentioned. (While the grandfather is "late lamented", his horse commands even greater immortality as "The never-to-be-forgotten Johnny" – De 207.) All the adults in the family enclave of "The Dead" are parentless, an epidemic situation in *Dubliners*, where even young adults seem devoid of parents, except for the fathers of Jimmy Doyle and John Corley and the separated parents of Polly Mooney. The genesis of this condition is apparent in the boyhood stories, where the protagonist of "The Sisters" and "Araby" lives instead with an aunt and uncle, while not even such surrogate parents are as much as mentioned in "An Encounter".

The extent to which the boy's parents are refined out of existence is made all the more poignant by the negative evidence, particularly in "The Sisters", where death is the immediate subject matter. There is ample time even in this brief narrative for the death of Father Flynn to evoke recollections in the boy of the death of his own parents (should he have been aware of the instances of their dying) or the condition of their being dead (should he have been too young when it actually happened). Instead, there is a vacuum, as if those deaths were too remote for his conscious comparison, or a blocked passage of thought would not allow the boy's mind to consider the trauma of the past. The psychological gnomon in "The Sisters" has two faces: that which shows itself in the first half of the story, as the protagonist actively investigates his reactions to the death of the priest, and that which hides itself in the second half, as he abdicates his function as active reactor and allows the events of the priest's death to unfold themselves "objectively", ghost-writing on the *tabula rasa* of his mind, to which he adds no marginal notations. By failing to comment on the conversation between his aunt and Eliza Flynn, by refusing to allow himself to think critically of the tenor of their talk, the boy not only succumbs to a form of mental paralysis, but also "disappears" from the scene (like Nannie in her deafness and fatigue), abstracted from the parallelogram.

"IMMOBILISED IN SPACE, REMOBILISED IN AIR"

The stage direction for the *gnomon* is quite specific, "the word gnomon in the Euclid" (Si 9) – some of Joyce's indicators are left vague, some self-explanatory, some pointedly marked. Yet even the Euclidian gnomon is self-reflexive and the gnomonics of *Dubliners* are of parallel possibilities: "the remainder of a parallelogram after the removal of a similar parallelogram containing one of its corners" suggests both absence (removal) and presence (remainder), that which has been taken away and that which survives. Both conditions are constantly operative in *Dubliners* and both germane to the technic of the volume. The presumably orphaned boy of the book's "Telemachiad" is the remaining factor in a construction that has lost the initial term of its construct: in his two "social" situations in "The Sisters" he is the uncomfortable fourth corner (uncommunicative when his aunt, uncle and Old Cotter discuss the death of Father Flynn, and when his aunt, Eliza and Nannie conduct a dismal wake at the bier). Whereas in the first instance he comments silently to himself, in the second he has given up even that degree of participation, so that totally abstracted he silently observes a parallelogram consisting of his aunt, the two Flynn sisters and the dead man. In the "Nostos" of *Dubliners*, "The Dead", some of the living return home, constantly casting their shadows over those dead that have been removed from the box stage of the Morkans' residence (itself a corner transplanted from the original house in Stoney Batter), and in turn are shadows themselves of those who haunt the corners of the rooms.

The "Odyssey" proper of *Dubliners* (stories four to fourteen) contains numerous instances of spiritual *legerdemain*, inexact substitutions, substances that cast no shadows, and frames that enclose no solid constructs. Eveline's rooms are mysteriously invaded by dust despite her weekly efforts to eliminate the accumulation – just as "the evening invade[s] the avenue" (Ev 36) as she watches from her window. She has chosen to replace the dusty air of Dublin with the clean air of Buenos Ayres, removing herself from an area in which she cannot prevent constant intrusions. "Down far in the avenue she could hear a street organ playing" (Ev 39–40) – a further uninvited invasion of her thoughts: and the familiar "air" conjures up an involuntary memory of her promise to her dying mother. The dead mother has been replaced by Blessed Margaret Mary Alacoque (temporarily, Eveline assumes, but the resolution of the story makes it a permanent replacement). Eveline, of late, has become a substitute for her missing brothers (Ernest now dead and Harry "in the church decorating business . . . nearly always down somewhere in the country" – Ev 38) as the recipient of her father's wrath. Should she manage to escape, she would undoubtedly be replaced in the victim's position by the young siblings whom she promised her mother she would protect – as a surrogate mother. "Ernest had been her favourite" (Ev 39), but he was no longer in the equation, his place miraculously taken by a sailor named Frank, "very kind, manly, open-hearted" (Ev 38), assuredly earnest.

In the invaded rooms of her mind Eveline Hill deconstructs the substance of the Dublin dwelling that she visualizes abandoning:

> Home! She looked round the room, reviewing all its familiar objects which she had dusted once a week for so many years, wondering where on earth all the dust came from. Perhaps she would never see again those familiar objects from which she had never dreamed of being divided –

and reconstructs it in her imagination at the other end of the world: "But in her new home, in a distant unknown country, it would not be like that. Then she would be married, she – Eveline" (Ev 37). The assumption that "She would not be treated as her mother had been" (Ev 37) is a chancy one, predicated on a false syllogism: after all, her mother had also been married and none the less had been badly treated. The ghost of the "melancholy air of Italy" (Ev 40) returns to project her memories back to her mother: the projection forward to her new life is consequently censored in her thoughts, the memories obviously instrumental in preventing her from boarding the ship. Adept at handling the Dublin market crowds on her own *terra cognita* ("holding her black leather purse tightly in her hand as she elbowed her way through the crowds and returning home late under her load of provisions" – Ev 38), she rebels against the "swaying crowd in the station at the North Wall" (Ev 40), and refuses to be pushed along toward that "distant unknown country," apparently opting for the Devil That You Know.

"Things Above Are Mirrored in Things Below" notes the oft-quoted precept from *The Emerald Tablets* of Hermes Trismegistus (Joyce's version in *Finnegans Wake* reads: "The tasks above are as the flasks below, saith the emerald canticle of Hermes" – FW 263.21–2), the mundane not so much negating the ethereal as corresponding to it. Eveline's successful manoeuvres through her neighbourhood market suggests one of the few instances in which she holds her own against a sea of trouble, tangible obstacles unlike the intangible dust. Her youthful counterpart in "Araby" also attempted to buck the tide of a similar environment, concentrating on the phantasm of Mangan's sister rather than the necessity of doing the shopping:

> Her image accompanied me even in places the most hostile to romance. On Saturday evenings when my aunt went marketing I had to go to carry some of the parcels. We walked through the flaring streets, jostled by drunken men and bargaining women, amid the curses of labourers, the shrill litanies of shop-boys who stood on guard by barrels of pigs' cheeks, the nasal chanting of street-singers, who sang a *come-all-you* about O'Donovan Rossa, or a ballad about the troubles in our native land. These noises converged in a single sensation of life for me: I imagined that I bore my chalice safely through a throng of foes.
>
> (Ar 31)

The boy assumes himself to be above the battle; Eveline persists as a vital part of it. She has temporarily accepted the hostility of her home, where she fought her father for the money with which to shop, and engaged herself in the pursuit of her provisions; the boy has been wrenched away from his romantic isolation to carry the aunt's purchases. Eveline's mundane black leather purse is mirrored in the ethereal chalice, and although he envisions himself as a romantic knight templar, the shouts of the shop-boys are to them their own plebian "litanies".

Like Eveline Hill, Jimmy Doyle also has only a single extant parent, but no mention is made of the significance, if any, of the missing mother. In his own life his father has undergone a major transformation, from merely a "butcher in Kingstown" to an entrepreneur "rich enough to be alluded to in the Dublin newspapers as a merchant prince" (Af 43). But in his change of status Mr Doyle has had to remove a part of himself which would no longer fit the new configuration: having "begun life as an advanced Nationalist", he "had modified his views early" (Af 43). The transformation that Jimmy himself undergoes during the one-day duration of "After the Race" is an ironic reverse image of his father's rise to wealth, especially ironic since Jimmy "has a respect for his father's shrewdness in business matters" (Af 45). As much as he would want to emulate his father's success by investing his patrimony in the automobile enterprise of his continental acquaintances, he loses it instead in a reckless evening of card-playing. The flaw in his procedure becomes apparent when he drunkenly and angrily adopts the role that his father had so prudently discarded. The presence of the Englishman Routh goads him into "advanced Nationalist views", so that "Jimmy, under generous influences, felt the buried zeal of his father wake to life within him" (Af 46). Here in Kingstown Harbour, within a stone's throw of the location of his father's first butcher shop, the son brings the family fortune full circle, or at least loses a significant part of it.

The card game results in Routh's victory and Doyle's defeat, and all the while, looming behind the action is the shadowy presence of the prudent Hungarian Villona, a calm and cautious musician whom Jimmy would have done well to imitate, abstaining from the card game and refusing to risk financial loss. The parallel position becomes obvious once the political perspective is enlarged: as we know from the Arthur Griffith pamphlet mentioned in *Ulysses* (for which Leopold Bloom is credited as ghost-writer), historically Hungary stands in mediate relation to Austria as Ireland does to England. In his zeal Jimmy Doyle has failed to credit the significant shadow cast by Villona, his ideal other self, until it is too late:

The cabin door opened and he saw the Hungarian standing in a shaft of grey light:
— Daybreak, gentlemen! (Af 48)

THE DISTANCE BETWEEN TWO POINTS

Whereas the geometric pattern formed by the time of the discourse in "After the Race" (from Doyle *père*'s origins to Doyle *fils*'s rude awakening) executes a full circle, the shape of the narrative (from the Naas Road into Dublin and out again to Kingstown Harbour) arcs like a campaniform crested in the centre of Dublin, where Mr Doyle made his money and the Doyles now live. The specifics are kept vague (Jimmy's house is somewhere just north of the Bank of Ireland), but the general line is carefully circumscribed. In "Two Gallants" the details are so precise as to graph the routes taken by the protagonists, especially Lenehan's lone stroll elliptically through central Dublin. His peregrinations mark three distinct orbits of increasing greater circumference with each excursion, and although he often retraces his steps along one side of a previous route, each of the three swathes that he cuts through Dublin topography creates a separate parallelogram contiguous with one of the others.

Entry into the Dublin maze is effected in the company of Corley, a man of straight and direct approaches. They saunter down into the heart of the city, cut east on Nassau Street, south on Kildare, east again on the north of the Green, until Corley makes contact with his slavey a short block south on the Hume Street corner. Lenehan then follows them till they board their tram and begins his solitary meanderings through the streets. North on Merrion Street and the west side of Merrion Square and west on Clare and Leinster Streets brings him back to the corner of Kildare and Nassau, completing the first circumambulation of a small parallelogram.

Even before reaching Kildare Street and the spot where he saw the harpist playing "Silent, O Moyle", Lenehan realizes himself responding to the sweetness of that "unheard music", an echo vestigial within him of the harpist's song – an auditory gnomon. But as he passes the place itself in front of the Kildare Club where the harpist stood, there is no mention of either the harpist still being there or Lenehan aware of the significance of the location. The narrative concerns itself with Lenehan's absorption of and with the music: "The air which the harpist had played began to control his movements. His softly padded feet played the melody while his fingers swept a scale of variations idly along the railings after each group of notes" (Tw 56). The railings here are along the Duke's Lawn, which means that Lenehan has not yet reached the point of origin, yet the next sentence finds him already heading west on St Stephen's Green South, a mental ellipsis parallel to Stephen's gnomonic visit to the Gouldings in Proteus. Even Lenehan's obtruding thoughts are as silent as the Moyle.

By heading north on Grafton Street Lenehan approaches the corner of Nassau Street and completes his second parallelogram, of greater extension than the first but also containing a portion of his previous walk with Corley, as if corroborating Corley's malicious suspicion when he asked, "Are you trying to get inside me?" (Tw 54). Only the third and most exorbitant of the three parallelograms is constructed exclusively of four sides of isolated and individualized walking by Lenehan, its first long side completed when he returns to a point at Rutland Square, where some time before he and Corley were coming down the hill. *"If Judas go forth tonight it is to Judas his steps will tend"*, Stephen Dedalus had mused (SC 1043–4), and as if his intention is to avoid any such confrontation, Lenehan turns sharp left at the Square, along a street that is never named in the text but where he discovers a "poor-looking shop" (Tw 57) for his meagre meal. In a narrative in which so many of the street names are meticulously catalogued, every one of them known to have strong associations with the British hegemony in Ireland, the silent but ghostly significance of this "dark quiet street" with its "sombre look" (Tw 57) is a gnomonic omission. Lenehan has wandered into Great Britain Street, where Father Flynn had lived – and died.

Once inside the food shop Lenehan finds himself a fourth corner in what had previously been an equilateral triangle. Seating himself opposite "two work-girls and a mechanic" he is obviously out of place, but "To appear natural he pushed his cap back on his head and planted his elbows on the table. The mechanic and the two work-girls examined him point by point before resuming their conversation in a subdued voice" (Tw 57). The uneasy alliance of the four delineates Lenehan as the odd man out, but in his thoughts he divorces himself from the parallelogram in order to conjure up an avatar, a married self seated at his hearth with a wife who finances his new incarnation. He has abstracted himself into his fantasy; then he abandons the field entirely to begin his wandering once again.

His next real encounter is with his own kind. He has since turned south on Capel Street and east on Dame Street where he comes upon two friends with whom he stops to talk. The subject turns to a fourth friend, a mysterious "Mac" whom one of them had seen on Westmoreland Street (the fourth side of the present geographic configuration that began with Great Britain, Capel and Dame Streets), and whom Lenehan had seen the night before in a pub. The shadowy Mac, his name only a hint of the full appellation, is here, there, everywhere, seen "an hour before" in one place and "the night before" (Two 58) in another, and the rumour that he might have won some money at billiards seems to make his present whereabouts of some importance. But nothing comes of it.

When Lenehan arrives at Grafton Street he has completed his third rhomboidal diagrammatic wandering, and a glance at the College of Surgeons clock tells him that time too has run out – he rushes forward toward his reunion with Corley. Now the basic quest for the gnomon begins: what has been lurking behind the Corley-Lenehan conspiracy has been kept from the reader, since the overheard part of their conversation remained ambiguous and no clear statement of intention ever intruded into Lenehan's thoughts. The elusiveness of the quest is accentuated as Lenehan's anxiety mounts: he focuses on an anticipated entity that does not exist ("kept his gaze fixed on the part from which he expected to see Corley and the young woman return"). What he sees is emptiness ("His eyes searched the street; there was no sign of them"), but he persists ("He strained his eyes as each tram stopped") until he concludes that they have eluded him ("They must have gone home by another way" – Tw 59). When they do materialize, a significant eclipse blocks his view: Corley's "broad figure hid hers from view for a few seconds and then she reappeared running up the steps" (Tw 60). With success in sight Lenehan now finds Corley purposely evasive, but he presses on and is finally vouchsafed a glimpse of the missing element, the yearned-for grail for which the knight had quested: "he extended a hand towards the light and, smiling, opened it slowly to the gaze of his disciple. A small gold coin shone in the palm" (Tw 60).

The overall gnomonic presence in "The Boarding House" is anchored in a familial parallelogram among the Mooneys: when Mr Mooney was abstracted from the pattern a vacuum was created into which Bob Doran unconsciously drifted against his will and better judgement. Changes have been rampant: the daughter of a butcher and the wife of a butcher, Mrs Mooney has become a boarding-house keeper; her daughter, once a typist, has been withdrawn from her job and is resident in the boarding-house; her son has been transformed into "a hard case" (Bo 62); and her discarded husband is now a bailiff's man. From Spring Garden the remaining three Mooneys have been transplanted to Hardwicke Street, where the missing Mooney received "neither money nor food nor house-room" (Bo 61). The newly reconstituted trio might have held their own had the father not imposed himself on Polly where she worked: once she has been removed from the corn-factor's office, her only option is marriage, and into that gap falls the timid Bob Doran. When the trap snaps shut, he has only one way out, by going over the wall, but he sees himself removed from his good job, and rather than risk that, he capitulates. One ironic aspect of the new, enforced pattern involves a future glimpse of Bob Doran in *Ulysses*, where, as a perennial drunk married to Polly, he has brought the circle to closure, replacing her drunken father in the quadrilateral equation, and probably as out of a job as his father-in-law.

"AS I WALKED OUT ONE EVENING . . . "

The next three *Dubliners* stories track the three central figures as they venture forth to encounter reality, not for the millionth time, as Stephen Dedalus intends at the end of *A Portrait*, but for the first time, "meeting robbers, ghosts, giants", etc. Of the three, Little Chandler is the most optimistic that the evening will be eventful: he comes armed with an image of himself as "T. Malone Chandler", poet "of the Celtic school". His armature is illusory, however, his armour-plating threadbare: crossing the Liffey he has his moment of inspiration when he views the houses huddled like tramps, and he wonders whether his ability to perceive the essential substance beneath a shadowy façade could be transmuted into original poetry, further speculating whether "Gallaher might be able to get it into some London paper for him" (Li 73). Before long Chandler has already glimpsed the English reviews of his volume of poems, almost unaware that an important solid entity has evaporated: the poems themselves. In meeting Gallaher (the robber – "he got mixed up in some shady affair, some money transaction"; the ghost – through absence in London for eight years; the giant – in Chandler's estimation: "Ignatius Gallaher of the London Press!" – Li 72), he seems to realize that this avatar of himself is someone he could never have become, nor would want to become, yet he is unsure whether he is relieved or all the more despondent at his pronounced inability to evolve into anything other than this insignificant self. His attempt to set himself on a new path, the reading of Byron presumably in preparation to becoming a Celtic Byron, proves shortlived. The attempt to read the first poem in the volume is interrupted, the poem truncated in the middle of the sixth line, another ellipsis disclosing the missing section of the structure.

In "Counterparts" (a title that reverberates with gnomonic import) Farrington Sober goes forth to encounter Farrington Drunk, yet the desired drunkenness by night shows itself to be as elusive as sober efficiency by day. Up until now he had been able to cover his tracks by several sleights-of-hand: providing himself with glasses of porter during working hours; keeping a cap in his pocket for the dash to the pub, while its surrogate remained on the hatrack; adding a caraway seed to disguise his breath. Eventually he will pawn his watch when money is otherwise unavailable, even to the extent of extracting six shillings from the pawn broker in lieu of the five offered. But on this decisive day the missing segments in his presumably ordered life in the offices of Crosbie and Alleyne have been consistently uncovered: letters are missing from the Delacour file; the Bodley and Kirwan contract cannot be copied out in time; *Bernard Bernard* has intruded on *Bernard Bodley*, the second Bernard a shadow of the first, the Bodley deleted entirely from the construct; the cashier cannot be relied on for an advance. When thoughts of riotous drinking consume him at his desk, he discovers that "His imagination had so abstracted him that his name was called twice [like *Bernard Bernard*] before he answered" (Co 91). Farrington has already been threatened with a negative report from the omnipresent Mr Alleyne to the mysteriously abstracted Mr Crosbie, a titular figure lurking somewhere in the wings.

The failure of the evening results from Farrington not being the man he claims to be, or perhaps not the man he was. With six shillings for capital and a good retort to capitalize on, he should have been able to get drunk enough to satisfy his desire for "a spell of riot" (Co 91), but falls short, paying for more drinks than he gets others to pay for, outclassed even in the telling of his own story by a surrogate raconteur from his own office, losing his title as strong man to an Englishman, and having to allow the "woman in the big hat" (Co 97) to escape him because his money had run out. His homecoming is also replete with portentous absences, "the kitchen empty and the kitchen fire nearly out" (Co 97). His wife has retreated to t1e chapel; the wrong son is there instead (in the dark he thinks that Tom is Charlie); no dinner is immediately available; and when our hero (himself a Noman without a given name) is on the verge of revenging himself on Tom, the boy offers to say a "Hail Mary" (Co 98), in lieu of the more appropriate "Our Father". But failure had always been in the offing for Farrington from the moment that a lacuna had settled into his narrated version of the retort to his boss: instead of faithfully repeating his comment, "I don't think, sir, he said, that that's a fair question to put to me" (Co 91), self-interest must have caused the omission of the pivotal word "sir" (Co 93).

Maria's journey has all the hallmarks of a familiar one, an almost ritualistic Halloween excursion, during which she anticipates few if any surprises – although she stresses her preference that she encounter Joe Donnelly sober rather than Joe Donnelly drunk: "He was so different when he took any drink" (Cl 100). The implication has an ironic extension when Maria approves of a total stranger, the "colonel-looking gentleman" on the tram, now maintaining that it was easy "to know a gentleman even when he has a drop taken" (Cl 102–3) – Joe is apparently a poor imitation of a gentleman. Maria (her missing last name a counterpart of Farrington's missing first name) is easily deceived by appearances, partly because she lives in a world in which "barmbracks seemed uncut; but if you went closer you would see that they had been cut into long thick even slices" (Cl 99); Maria "saw that every woman got her four slices" (Cl 101). Equilateral squares removed from a seemingly whole rhomboid imply both a completeness and unity that are misleading: Maria *never* gets the ring that has been baked into one of these slices, although Lizzie Fleming *always* assures her that she will. When Maria laughs, "the tip of her nose *nearly* met the tip of her chin"; she sits in the tram (the only seat available is the stool at the end; on the second tram the only seat is the one offered by the only gentleman), "her toes *barely* touching the floor" (Cl 101–2; emphasis added). Hailed as a peacemaker at the laundry, Maria has been a longtime failure in any attempt to make peace between Joe and his brother Alphy, despite having once been hailed as a "proper mother". In Joe Donnelly's household, however, there is a "stand-in" for the outcast brother, his nephew Alphy, apparently named for him when the brothers had still been at peace with one another.

That there are numerous gaps in Maria's life is obvious as the "Clay" narrative develops, and they are mirrored in the minutia of missing items in near-comic proportions: by giving away "one or two slips" from her plants (Cl 100) Maria is creating gnomonic patterns, which are expected to grow back and recomplete the pattern; by serving tea she disappoints Ginger Mooney, who would prefer "a sup of porter" (Cl 101). Later, she changes cake shops because "Downes's plumcake had not enough almond icing on top" (Cl 102), and then of course manages to lose the plumcake on the tram, having exchanged one tram for another. Offered stout or port she wants neither (Ginger Mooney should have come in her place), but Joe insists and she has to accept. First Joe cannot find the nutcracker and then cannot see the corkscrew (a missing corkscrew temporarily inhibits the "festivities" in the committee room). Mischievously presented with the clay during the divination game, Maria has it mysteriously withdrawn from her, replaced by a prayerbook – but still no ring.

The culmination of such lacunae comes with the singing of "I Dreamt that I Dwelt", when Maria fails to sing the second verse, superimposing a repeated rendition of the first on the empty space. Scrutiny of the deleted verse fails to unearth any excessively romantic elements in any way more potent that those in the first verse, leading to the conclusion that Maria has somehow become so sufficiently *fixed* on those elements in the first as to become a case of arrested development. Even her "minute" body corroborates that arrest ("In spite of its years she found it a nice tidy little body" – Cl 101), and her lack of maturity and adult sophistication makes her the butt of both condescension and mockery: there is no wedding cake in the offing for her and no ring. Even the assumption that a lack of maturation means a permanent stasis is unrealistic, since Maria's holds on both her position at the laundry and on life are tenuous. "Clay" as a Halloween ghost story portends more than it presents, as death is read in common garden clay and in a series of losses that leave very little left to lose.

No one maintains as tight a control on the status quo as Maria's successor, Mr James Duffy. By a monkish ordering of his life he allows for no chances of surprise, no vulnerable gaps in a solid façade, no expectation that can lead to disappointment. The route that he has carefully circumscribed for himself takes him from his room in Chapelizod to his bank in Baggot Street; lunch at Dan Burke's and dinner in "an eating-house in George's Street" (Pa 108–9) make his day fixed and predictable. Evenings are somewhat less structured, and when he finds himself an inappropriate bourgeois intellectual among hardheaded workmen at meetings of the Irish Socialist Party, he abstracts himself from a situation in which he does not properly fit. Music concerts are certainly more consistent with his life, until he chances to meet Mrs Sinico, a woman for whom a vacuum has been created because her ship's captain husband "was often away" (Pa 110). Introducing himself into the Sinico household, so as not to be meeting her surreptitiously, Duffy finds himself sailing under false colours, since the Captain assumes that he is courting the daughter ("he had dismissed his wife so sincerely from his gallery of pleasures that he did not suspect that anyone else would take an interest in her" – Pa 110). At least two interesting segments thus emerge from the Duffy/Mrs Sinico/Captain Sinico/Mary Sinico parallelogram.

As a construct "A Painful Case" is a narrative that contains as its centrepiece the newspaper item subheaded "A Painful Case" – the second title serving as an indicator pointing toward Mrs Sinico, but the overall title pointing unrelentingly toward James Duffy. The one case impinges on the other: what was relevant for Mrs Sinico is relevant for Mr Duffy. He is quick to read certain signs that disturb his equilibrium and lead to his rupture with her ("she had shown every sign of unusual excitement" – Pa 111). She in turn failed to heed the signals that warned her of danger: "The company had always taken every precaution to prevent people crossing the lines except by the bridges, both by placing notices in every station and by the use of patent spring gates at level crossings" (Pa 114). In the one case caution leads to stagnation; in the other indifference to caution results in self-destruction.

In the interim between dismissing her from his life and the end of her life, several self-contained sections of Duffy's highly ordered existence are deleted: "He kept away from concerts. . . . His father died; the junior partner of the bank retired" (Pa 112). On the night in which she died all other members of Mrs Sinico's immediate family are absent from her life: her husband "was not in Dublin at the time of the accident" and her daughter "was not at home until an hour after the accident" (Pa 114, 115). That "No blame attached to anyone" makes "blame" an active rather than a passive agent, and is as equally applicable to the exonerated engine-driver and the victim herself – and by extension to the innocent bank cashier who once "allowed himself to think that in certain circumstances he would rob his bank but, as the circumstances never arose, his life rolled out evenly – an adventureless tale" (Pa 109).

CHINESE BOXES

The three public life stories extend the structures and intensify the textures of the increasingly complex narratives that lead to "The Dead". Each of the last four stories assumes the proportions of a parallelepiped, as prismatic as they are parallelogrammatic, from which solid segments are deftly deleted as we watch certain forms take shape, and in which empty sections are enigmatically filled. In Tierney's election headquarters in "Ivy Day" the man himself never turns up, perhaps never really expected, himself a mere shadow of the Parnell politician to whose coat-tails he nominally adheres. Parnell himself is a shade of a shade, present primarily in a poem praised for its fine writing, but containing various qualities, like sincere appreciation, while obviously devoid of any aspect of fine writing. That Tierney is so unlike Parnell has allowed Wilkins, the Conservative candidate, to withdraw from the race (he is too exactly duplicated by Tierney), imposing his canvasser Crofton on the Nationalists, despite Crofton's discomfort among them. (In *Ulysses* he is "unnamed" by the collector of bad debts as "Crofter or Crofton . . . Crawford" (Cy 1589–91), but the unnamed collector opts for Crofter despite hearing him called Crofton, and later opts for "Crofton or Crawford" (Cy 1752) once Myles Crawford's name is mentioned.)

Some of the lines of demarcation, however, show themselves to be rather blurred than exact, so that the linear succession of parent and child rarely results in an actual duplication: Jack the caretaker complains of the dissoluteness and ingratitude of his son; Joe Hynes is declared not be "nineteen carat" (Iv 124), although his father is lionized ("Many a good turn he did in his day" – Iv 124); and Tierney is reduced to a "Mean little tinker" and a "Mean little shoeboy of hell" (Iv 123). In denigrating Tierney's origins Mr Henchy unintentionally poses the opposite equation: Tierney's father had kept a used-clothing shop and kept a bottle on hand for his Sunday morning cronies, while his son has become a publican selling drinks on a much larger scale. Nor is the parallel between King Edward VII and his mother devoid of irony: his profligate life is excused by Henchy, who encourages his visit to Ireland, all the more because of his annoyance that Queen Victoria has never deigned to make the voyage – although she actually visited Ireland on several occasions.

Disproportion in "Ivy Day" is often caused by the myopic sighting through the wrong end of the telescope, although some reversals are possible under the right circumstances. For the assembled canvassers, who are in the process of talking about their achievements but are certainly not out canvassing at the moment, the missing items are payment and promised drinks from Tierney's pub. As long as neither is forthcoming, their attitudes are jaundiced. As soon as the dozen bottles of stout make their belated appearance (even without the necessary corkscrew), the grievance about the missing money evaporates. And Henchy, who had suspected Joe Hynes of being a spy for the opposition, now praises him as a loyal Parnellite, having been markedly altered by the intrusion of a bottle of stout.

Over generous dollops of whisky Hoppy Holohan and Mrs Kearney sign a contract for the musical services of Kathleen Kearney at a series of concerts sponsored by the *Eire Abu* Society. Although these are the constants in the foreground, two variables lurk in the shadows. One is Mr Kearney, "sober, thrifty and pious", whose "conversation, which was serious, took place at intervals in his great brown beard" (Mo 137); the other is Mr Fitzpatrick, the secretary of the Society (Holohan is after all only the "assistant secretary" – Mo 136), with a "vacant smile" (Mo 140) that Mrs Kearney immediately finds irritating. As the events unfold, Holohan is progressively eliminated from the configuration just as the husband is kept well in the background, and even at the beginning Hoppy was easily eclipsed by the efficient Mrs Kearney filling a void ("it was Mrs Kearney who arranged everything" – Mo 136), so that no sooner is he challenged by her than Holohan effaces himself, deferring to his superior: "You'd better speak to Mr Fitzpatrick, said Mr Holohan distantly" (Mo 144). When confronted by her, Mr Fitzpatrick invokes (and immediately hides behind) an even vaster and more mysterious entity: "Mr Fitzpatrick, who did not catch the point at issue very quickly, seemed unable to resolve the difficulty and said that he would bring the matter before the Committee" (Mo 141). Mrs Kearney is understandably dubious about such an indeterminate body, although she withholds her sarcastic question, "And who is the *Cometty*, pray?" (Mo 141), but later vents her annoyance by challenging the existence of any such "invisible" body: "I haven't seen any Committee" (Mo 148). For its purposes of evading the angry Mrs Kearney, Fitzpatrick's elusive

Committee, like the "Society" for which it stands surrogate, has its very solidity in not being tangible.

"A Mother" is replete with several four-sided figures that are constantly losing their fourth sides. Initially there were to have been four concerts, but as the projected audiences failed to materialize, one of the performances was summarily cancelled. For the four concerts Kathleen Kearney was to have been paid eight guineas, but with one now voided, Mrs Kearney suspects that her daughter will not receive the full contracted fee. When she brings the matter to a confrontation, Mr Fitzpatrick gives her half the fee and promises the other half later, yet even the half offered is a shade off, pounds instead of guineas, so that for each of the pounds now in question a shilling has been shaved off: " – This is four shillings short" (Mo 147).

The mathematics of the story parallel its geometrics, as the equation reduces itself down to nothing. The redoubtable Mrs Kearney had counted on the formidable presence of her husband, the enormous shadow behind her to match Holohan's Fitzpatrick, and the great-bearded husband is marshalled for the showdown on the final evening. She had married him when the romantic young men did not manage to overcome the ivory-mannered defences she set up as a challenge. Now she is playing her trump against Fitzpatrick's high card, the *Cometty*: "She respected her husband in the same way as she respected the General Post Office, as something large, secure and fixed; and though she knew the small number of his talents she appreciated his abstract value as a male" (Mo 141). Mr Kearney, however, hardly succeeds in being effective, having long since had his masculine value abstracted from him by the ivory manners of his dominant wife, and in conflict with so abstract a quantity as the Committee he is powerless. Opposing forces line up as two pockets of contestants form:

> In one corner were Mr Holohan, Mr Fitzpatrick, Miss Beirne, two of the stewards, the baritone, the bass, and Mr O'Madden Burke.
> (Mo 147)

> In another corner of the room were Mrs Kearney and her husband, Mr Bell, Miss Healy and the young lady who had recited the patriotic piece.
> (Mo 148)

The proportions are already unequal, all the more so since one of the minority party is uncomfortable on Mrs Kearney's side: "Miss Healy wanted to join the other group but . . . " (Mo 148). When Mrs Kearney belittles Hoppy Holohan as "a great fellow fol-the-diddle-I-do", he in turn reduces her stature: "I thought you were a lady" (Mo 149). "After that Mrs Kearney's conduct was condemned on all hands" (Mo 149), and the disbalance of power is final. The parallelogram assumes its completed form, ejecting the intrusive Kearney contingent from its corner. The Kearneys retreat *en bloc* from the fray, although Mrs Kearney refuses to allow herself to be removed from the contour ("I'm not done with you yet, she said"), but Hoppy Holohan makes the removal complete: "But I'm done with you, said Mr Holohan" (Mo 149).

Many of the gnomonics of these stories are comic in their effects: abandoned plumcakes, misplaced nutcrackers and corkscrews, anticipated bottles of stout, fires that provide no light or heat, priests that look like actors, narrow gaps barely separating nose and chin, toes and floor, solid males who become mere shadows of their former selves, audiences composed of "paper", and unknown sopranos from London in "faded" dresses over "meagre" bodies (Mo 143). (Madam Glynn has the distinction of personifying both characteristics of the gnomon, that which is hidden and that which is prominently exposed: "The shadow took her faded dress into shelter but fell revengefully into the little cup behind her collarbone" – Mo 143.)

Nowhere are the gnomons more comic than in "Grace", where Tom Kernan's misstep on the pub lavatory stairs results in a piece of his tongue being gone. Mrs Kernan dreams up a fourth for the Holy Trinity; three comforters are unexpectedly augmented into a quadrumvirate; Pope Leo XIII is credited with extolling photography in verse (a photograph being a gnomonic presence long after the subject is gone); two so-called gentlemen accompanied Kernan on his drinking rounds, but evaporated when he took his misstep; McCoy has changed professional identities at least six times; Mr Harford is denounced as an "Irish Jew" (Gr 159) but shows up at the Catholic retreat, where Father Purdon sounds more like a businessman than a priest, delivering a non-sermon on an ambiguous text given in a translation that would rarely be acknowledged as accurate. To complete the picture, the party of five who materialize in the Gardiner Street church reconstitute themselves strategically in the only way that five can conform to a quadrilateral shape: "the party had settled down in the form of a quincunx" (Gr 172). McCoy is of course the odd man out (he "had tried unsuccessfully to find a place in the bench with the others" – Gr 172), so becomes the central point in the quincunx by sitting alone in the middle, with two in front of him and two behind.

The gnomons that abound in *Dubliners* – or would abound if they were not so blatantly missing – reflect the narrative strategies of the stories: absence of climactic instances, deleted resolutions of plot, inconclusive closures, inexact overlays of perception on the part of the participants, insufficient information about them. So Maria is devoid of her family name and Farrington his given name, and the boy in the first three stories has no names at all (although the boy in "An Encounter" at least is distinguished by not being named Smith). By contrast so trivial a character as the representative of the railway company at Mrs Sinico's inquest is fully equipped with a handle as proponderant as "H. B. Patterson Finlay". Nomenclature is in itself gnominic ("Sounds are impostures", Stephen Dedalus contends; "Like names" – so "What's in a name?" he asks – Eu 362–4), and Farrington is often referred to in the text as "The man", yet in losing his match with Weathers he is unmanned, reduced to Noman.

Many another male Dubliner is deprived of his full masculinity: Bob Doran at the hands of the Mooney women; Mr Kearney in the hands of a determined wife; Gabriel Conroy, self-styled Romantic Man, deflated by the intrusion into his life of the ghostly Michael Furey, a stripling long since dead who had long ago outdistanced him as a lover in a competition that Gabriel had never been aware of. Little Chandler, already on the outs with his wife because he had forgotten to bring home "the parcel of coffee from Bewley's" (Li 82), is further diminished in her eyes when she returns to find him unable to quiet the infant. Turning her back on her husband, "Giving no heed to him", she nullifies his existence by concentrating exclusively on the child, calling the baby "My little man! My little mannie!" (Li 85).

The word "gnomon" derives from the Greek, designating an "interpreter, discerner, pointer on a sundial, a carpenter's square". The most pointed indicators as such in *Dubliners* are the story titles, the first indications in each instance. The book title characterizes an entire population, and by internal reference a place of residence, yet the parts that stand for the whole are the handful of Dubliners actually delineated in the fifteen stories. Of the individual titles some pinpoint characters ("The Sisters", "Eveline", "Two Gallants", "A Mother"); others a place ("Araby", "The Boarding House", "Ivy Day in the Committee Room"); and several a condition ("A Painful Case", "Grace", "The Dead"). The directness of most of them is deceptive, but a handful are highly elliptical and ambiguous. Irony informs "Two Gallants", where gallantry is decidedly unobservable; that it is Ivy Day during the course of the political tale arranges for ironic contrast of a pervasive ideal with the diluted Parnellism of the canvassers. "Grace" as well is intentional overstatement, since few would consider either Kernan or any of the others in a state of grace despite their physical presence in church, and Kernan may more accurately be in a state of animated suspension. "Clay" offers various possibilities in the literal substance brought forth and withdrawn during the séance: its applicability to the malleable character of the unfortunate Maria and its symbolic import as a designation of death, prefigured as such in the Byron poem Chandler fails to read all the way through. "Counterparts" is itself a counter of various parts, contrasting Farrington with each of his adversaries throughout, from Mr Alleyne to Higgins to Weathers to son Tom, and extending laterally in counterpartite applicability to the Chandler of the preceding story, where "A Little Cloud" parallels the person of Little Chandler and a condition that marks him and affects him. That "The Sisters" deflects attention away from the dead priest to his surviving sisters indicates the method of narrative counterpoint, as is also the case in "The Dead", in which two sisters also figure prominently. The viability of interexchanging the titles of the opening and closing stories offers a circular construct for *Dubliners*, a cycle that Joyce artistically quadratures in the gnomonic parallel structures, squaring the circle, encircling the numerous squares, creating "Encounterparts".

3

Symbolic Systems: Correspondences in the Tales

. . . symbolism or idealism, the supreme quality of beauty being a light from some other world, the idea of which the matter is but the shadow, the reality of which it is but the symbol.

(AP 213)

There was grace and mystery in her attitude as if she were a symbol of something. He asked himself what is a woman standing on the stairs in the shadow, listening to distant music, a symbol of.

(De 210)

The distance between Stephen Dedalus, reconstituting an aesthetics based on Aquinas for an indifferent Lynch, and Gabriel Conroy, experiencing an aesthetic moment confused with sexual adoration of the entranced Gretta, is allied to the distance between literature and the market-place, both of which Stephen is aware of and Gabriel involved with. Stephen concedes that his definitions are in the realm of "literary talk", and differentiates "beauty" ("in the sense which the word has in literary tradition") from that of "the marketplace", where "it has another sense" (AP 213). For Gabriel the apprehension of beauty leads also into the aesthetic realm, positing a symbolic painting of that which he immediately perceives, but a work of art that he has no intention of undertaking, never having adequately interpreted the symbolic significance. In giving the painting a title, "Distant Music", he translates the experience into a potential commodity that would have relevance within the market-place. Although a teacher of literature and a reviewer of books, Gabriel has moved his aesthetics outside the area of language, whereas Stephen is especially specific in establishing the distance between words "used according to the literary tradition" and "according to the tradition of the marketplace" (AP 188). The literary domain of Joyce's *Dubliners*, however, exists within both traditions, in the bridge between them and the constant interaction between them.

In characterizing the style of *Dubliners* as that of "scrupulous meanness", Joyce took into consideration the duplicity of language, even the triviality of language. That "small sharp stone" that is the etymological discomfiting device in a "scruple" has its immediate sounding in the first story when Father Flynn is described as having been "too scrupulous always" (Si 17), but there is no indication that his sisters really appreciate him for that tendency. Joyce's scrupulous meanness in the execution of *Dubliners* focused on two aspects of the operative noun: for that quality which is without embellishment or elaboration and for the state that centres exactly between the possible extremes. Flaubert's *mot juste* is scrupulously mean – as is the careful calculation of copper coins.

To practice such rigid economy of style requires that things as well as words serve multiple purposes, that the sparse outlay of coin of the realm buys several items simultaneously. Ordinary household gadgets, therefore, take on extended significance in a context in which they are required to cover several areas. That relatively mundane object, the handy corkscrew, present in "Clay" but unseen by the misty-eyed Joe Donnelly, absent but much considered by the thirsty in "Ivy Day", may have no extended meaning in its shape and size and spiral contours, but does in focusing on Donnelly's capacity to commiserate with the pathetic Maria and in mirroring Tierney's indifference to the needs of his campaign workers.

"ONCE BY INADVERTENCE, TWICE BY DESIGN"

A corkscrew's capacity to disappear from view (ghostly even in its presence) or not to appear at all (eloquent as a ghost through absence) is in direct relationship to the beholder and user. Acceptable as an item one would expect to find in the Donnelly household, it might not have an equally relevant place in the committee room, but should have been brought in with the bottles it is expected to open. " – Here, boy! said Mr Henchy, will you run over to O'Farrell's and ask him to lend us a corkscrew – for Mr Henchy, say. Tell him we won't keep it a minute" (Iv 128): by this stratagem the implement is procured, and as good as his word, Henchy sends it back once it has done its service. The belated arrival of Lyons and Crofton, however, once more necessitates a means of drawing corks from bottles: the pub boy is no longer present to be sent to O'Farrell's and Henchy obviously has no intention of going himself. Instead, he devises a new stratagem. By placing the bottles on the hob, he allows the pressure to build up in the stout so that the corks are eventually ejected. With a momentous *Pok!* Lyons's cork flies out, but Crofton's is somewhat delayed, and by the time it does *Pok!*, it propels Crofton forward just as he is being asked his opinion of Parnell. His "politic" reply ("Our side of the house respects him because he was a gentleman" – Iv 133) is applauded excessively by Mr Henchy, whose mood has much improved with the drink. Henchy is now equally enthusiastic about Joe Hynes, who also reappears, and offers him a drink as well. (Henchy has expanded his approval to both sides of the political aisle, from Crofton's Conservatives to Hynes's Socialists, on the basis of a sup of stout.) For Hynes's benefit the charade of the non-existent corkscrew gets played out once again by Henchy, and his magical performance is again employed, but the third *Pok!* goes unnoticed by a Hynes lost in emotional revery over Parnell. All for the want of an inconsequential corkscrew.

Many a single object in a *Dubliners* story looms large as having more than mere verisimilitudinistic weight (Maria's plumcake for example), but the parallel roles of a pair of corkscrews in a pair of stories reveal a figure of faint design in the carpet. Maria's plum-cake, singular in appearance but multivalent in its disappearance, qualifies as more than just an emphatic assertion: it carries the poss-ibility of symbolic overtones as well. Maria had changed trams at Nelson's Pillar, cake-shopping in the interval in Earl and Henry Streets, an area in which two other spinsters have their outing in *Ulysses*, at least in the narrative created by Stephen Dedalus while in the same locale, "*A Pisgah Sight of Palestine* or *The Parable of The Plums*" (Ae 1057–8). If we regard the plumstones cast on to the Sackville Street roadway by vestals atop Nelson's Pillar as onanistic and sterile, then by analogy the cake baked with ripe plums denotes fertility in sharp distinction to Maria's spinsterish existence. The loss of the plumcake, under suspect circumstances considering that the "colonel-looking gentleman" flustered her to the extent that she "favoured him with demure nods and hems" (Cl 103), corroborates Maria's role as an infertile crone doomed to an empty and futureless existence. Her subsequent action, once she is aware of the absence of the plumcake, establishes the direction of the symbolic import as she tends to place the blame on the younger generation (who balk at allowing the blame to attach to them), rather than face the importance of the effect on her of the "elderly gentleman" (Cl 102).

As if in retaliation, the children turn the tables and play their symbolic prank: those presumed to have purloined the golden plums of fertility for themselves in turn award the symbol of death in the mysterious rites, changing the stakes in the game. Divination rituals are in their very nature symbolic, but the benign form "officially" played at the Donnellys' and presided over by the adults in the household involves only the prospects of marriage, of a voyage or of a clerical vocation, each of these "positive" possibilities already suspect in a land in which poverty and lack of opportunity determine many a young person's future. The "next-door girls" (Cl 105) are the ones apparently responsible for adding a fragmented entity to the carefully prescribed tripartite contours of the fortune-telling, and they apparently "guide" Maria directly toward her doom. Overlapping the double-design of the "Clay" title is an echo of the sound of Chandler reading from the Byron elegy, where the singular meaning of clay in the grave of the dead Margaret reinforces the behaviour of the audacious girl from next-door (Chandler in this instance attempting to ignore his crying child, the future generation):

Within this narrow cell reclines her clay,
That clay where once ... (Li 84)

Here the ellipsis is the absence that has its gnomonic completion in Maria's clay, positing a combined (Blessed) Margaret Maria.

The technique of double-design unfolds throughout the weave of the fifteen *Dubliners* tales in a series of subtle links, some conveniently spaced together but others widely separated. That there is no fire laid on in the Flynn sitting room is unremarkable, considering that it is a July evening ("we all gazed at the empty fire-place" – Si 15), but it becomes more noticeable with the unnecessary repetition ("she . . . gazed into the empty grate for some time without speaking" – Si 17), especially in a story steeped in death and loss, poverty and vacancy: it is not the fireplace that is the object observed, but its emptiness. Yet a fire does exist on this July evening at the boy's residence ("Old Cotter was sitting at the fire, smoking, when I came downstairs to supper" – Si 9), and by analogy a fire also exists in the grate in "Ivy Day", and a necessary one considering the cold, wet day, but it is a paltry fire that fails to provide either light or warmth. A further link exists with these "failed" fires in "Counterparts", Farrington arriving home to discover "the kitchen fire nearly out", attacking his son for his negligence: "I'll teach you to let the fire out!" (Co 97, 98). Thrice-by-design the pattern emerges of an empty grate and a dying fire and a weak, inadequate one that Mr Henchy hopes to reactivate, pleading, "For the love of God, Jack, bring us a bit of coal" (Iv 123). To balance the demise of the fire needed to provide Farrington's late supper, the opening of "Clay" offers Maria's institutional kitchen at the laundry, where "The fire was nice and bright" (Cl 99), as well as the Donnelly hearth, where Maria is urged toward a seat "by the fire" (Cl 104).

The cold darkness that dominates Tierney's headquarters derives primarily from the paralytic condition of Ireland's hemaplegia of the will, rather than from an unusual cold snap in October. The impotent old caretaker rakes the cinders, spreads them evenly, fans the fire, and produces hardly enough flame to light up his own countenance. "Is this a Freemasons' meeting?" (Iv 120), asks Joe Hynes facetiously upon entering the office. When Henchy enters he walks "over quickly to the fire, rubbing his hands as if he intended to produce a spark from them" (Iv 122). Father Keon's entrance in the dark makes him almost unrecognizable to those assembled in the room, and Henchy offers to light the priest's way down the dark stairs. The denizens of the committee room have grown accustomed to the gloom, and to a series of other inconveniences, but the boy in "Araby" realizes himself to have entered not the magical wonderland of an oriental bazaar, but an atmosphere where "the greater part of the hall was in darkness" (Ar 34), the gnomon consuming its parallelogram. He soon hears "a voice call from one end of the gallery that the light was out. The upper part of the hall was now completely dark" (Ar 35). It is just such a darkness that descends on Mr Duffy on the evening in which he reads the news of Mrs Sinico's death, a darkness that deepens and intensifies, "cold and gloomy": "She seemed to be near him in the darkness" at first, but then "He could not feel her near him in the darkness nor her voice touch his ear" (Pa 117). Rather than merely an absence of light, darkness becomes an operative presence for Duffy and the young boy and the canvassers.

Symbolic correspondences in *Dubliners* are not always of such ominous import; comic juxtaposition occasionally plays its part as well. That the boy in "The Sisters" mysteriously dreams of Persia seems almost gratuitous (literary license), and that his counterpart in "Araby" attends a bazaar with a corresponding Middle-Eastern designation owes its origins to an actual event in Dublin (historical verisimilitude), but these set up a parallel that is completed many tales later when it is revealed that a frustrated Miss Devlin ("A Mother") consoles herself by consuming quantities of Turkish Delight. Other associations are almost inexplicably tenuous in design, although obviously quite direct: Father Flynn's paralytic condition causes "constant showers of snuff" to give "his ancient priestly garments their green faded look" (Si 12); "When he smiled he used to uncover his big discoloured teeth" (Si 13). When the boy in "An Encounter" crosses the Liffey he examines "the foreign sailors to see had any of them green eyes", but only one sailor approximates his expectation, "whose eyes could have been called green" (En 23). He later encounters the pederast, however, "shabbily dressed in a suit of greenish-black", who, when he smiled, showed "great gaps in his mouth between his yellow teeth" (En 24, 25). It is not until after the "queer old josser" has gone off to perform his private, mysterious rite that the boy notices his "bottle-green eyes peering at me" (En 27), eyes that correspond to the boy's confused notion, but no longer something that he actively seeks. The clothes and teeth obliquely correspond to those of Father Flynn, the priest who taught "how complex and mysterious were certain institutions of the Church" (Si 13): when the pederast indulges in his flagellant fantasy, the boy interprets it "as if he were unfolding some elaborate mystery" (En 27). The links that bind the priest and the "josser" in the complex contextual structure transcend mere symbolic correspondence and develop a network of associations into a symbolic system.

"A JIGSAW PUZZLE OF NEEDLES AND PINS AND BLANKETS AND SHINS"

On numerous occasions *Dubliners* presents a series of solitary symbols, exclusively or primarily attached to the thematic structuring of a particular story. If symbolic denotation were an exact science, Joyce could claim that in *Dubliners* he attempted every possible kind of experimentation and rarely if ever duplicated his symbolic species: the harp in "Two Gallants" (political representation); the houses along the Liffey in "A Little Cloud" (poetic association); the blind street in "Araby" (thematic designation); the dust in "Eveline" (reverberative impact and contrast); the red light in "Grace" (irony); the gold coin in "Two Gallants" (epiphanic revelation). Even the "twice by design" instances are never quite the same in each case, and can be as diversely separated as Old Cotter "talking of faints and worms . . . his endless stories about the distillery" (Si 10) and Duffy in Chapelizod living within the shadow of a "disused distillery" (Pa 107). The Cotter allusion is faintly comic and plays upon the boy's exasperation with the worthless old man; for Duffy the proximity of the disused distillery that he can view from his window is an almost welcome facet of his chosen life in the unpretentious suburb, but takes on the aura of the conspiring landscape with his full awareness of the horror of the Sinico Case. Together with the "cheerless evening", the failing light, the "lonely road", the "gaunt trees", the "bleak alleys", the "cold night" (Pa 115–17), the gross workmen in the pub and the fornicating couples in the park, the "empty distillery" (Pa 115) as a symbol of absence and disuse parallels Mrs Sinico"s life and Mr Duffy's mood.

Inobtrusively established at the beginning of "A Painful Case", the distillery assumes panoramic proportions in the closing section, whereas the snow in "The Dead" persists throughout the narrative as an entity constantly capable of symbolic overtones. The exuberant and dynamic quality of the snowfall is fixed immediately with Gabriel's entrance: he wears it as if it were his emblem, "like a cape on the shoulders of his overcoat", emitting "a cold fragrant air from out-of-doors" (none the less he makes his prophetic announcement, "I think we're in for a night of it" – De 177). Twice during the evening in the overly warm atmosphere of the Morkan party Gabriel is lured both physically and mystically by the bracing out-of-doors allure of the snow: when he leans against the cold window and imagines the snow in Phoenix Park capping the Wellington Monument, and again at the dinner table when he recapitulates his imaginings with a yearning identification with the heroic figure immortalized with a phallic monument. (Later, he identifies with a very different heroic figure, the snow-capped Daniel O'Connell: "Good-night, Dan, he said gaily" – De 214).

There is obvious irony in his rapport with the snow, since it is actually Gretta who is identified unstintingly with that natural phenomenon: " – But as for Gretta there, said Gabriel, she'd walk home in the snow if she were let" (De 180). Gabriel, after all, welcomes the snow while carefully protected by overcoat and goloshes.

Snow symbolism undergoes a metamorphic reversal in "The Dead", paralleling the narrative process throughout. The two internal indicators, Gabriel's contemplations of the snowcapped memorial, contrast importantly with the overheated atmosphere of the Morkan soirée, with the "hot work" of carving the goose (De 197) and the recollection of the bottle-makers at their furnace ("Is the fire hot, sir?" – De 213). As the evening's activities wind down, the doors are opened to the cold outside, to awareness of the "snow-covered quay" (De 206) and the ominous note sounded that Bartell D'Arcy fears the effect of the snowy weather on his sick throat:

> – They say, said Mary Jane, we haven't had snow like it for thirty years; and I read this morning in the newspapers that the snow is general all over Ireland.
> – I love the look of snow, said Aunt Julia sadly.
> – So do I, said Miss O'Callaghan. I think Christmas is never really Christmas unless we have the snow on the ground. (De 211)

In this light conversation the tensions are set that will determine the rise and fall of Gabriel's mood during the course of the dénouement in the Gresham.

That it had actually stopped snowing during the course of the party on Usher's Island has gone unstated: Gabriel had come in bearing evidence of falling snow, but the emphasis thereafter was on a snow-covered landscape. Excitement and enthusiasm regarding the snow had been maintained by Gabriel's attitude of almost lustful embracing of the snowy condition, but by stark contrast the journey on foot in search of a cab reveals that "It was slushy underfoot; and only streaks and patches of snow lay on the roofs, on the parapets of the quay and on the area railing" (De 212–13). Only Gabriel's erotic anticipations sustain the glorious aspect of the snow-decked landscape ("Good-night, Dan") in the face of the "objective" presentation of the setting, consistent with Gretta's mood and "The Lass of Aughrim": "The lamps were still burning redly in the murky air and, across the river, the palace of the Four Courts stood out menacingly against the heavy sky" (De 213). When Gabriel's mood is eventually darkened by the revelations regarding Michael Furey, he faces that alternative world outside his window: "A few light taps upon the pane made him turn to the window. It had begun to snow again." For him now the snow is "silver and dark" (De 223) and his thoughts persistently on death, on graveyards and the moribund, re-emphasizing that "the newspapers were right", that "snow was general all over Ireland" (De 223). A morbid *Todentanz* of snowflakes fall as Gabriel's "soul swooned slowly as he heard the snow falling faintly through the universe and faintly falling, like the descent of their last end, upon all the living and the dead" (De 224) – the newspaper never mentioned the living and the dead.

The repeated use of symbolic overtones and connectives in *Dubliners* suggests the possibility of a symbolic system at work throughout, informing all of the stories and establishing a unity along symbolistic lines to supplement the thematic and spatial unities inherent in this collection of compacted narratives. The unifying spirit that weaves its way almost imperceptibly through *Dubliners* is the aura of the Holy Ghost (often more notably in its absence than its presence), and a consequent augmentation of the paralytic and simoniac themes. That Catholic life in Dublin remains sadly untouched by the spirit that should inform its religious essence is apparent in every group situation and every individual case history. Like James Duffy these Dubliners live empty existences unhaunted, unaffected and spiritlessly alone, and when they die, it is like Father Flynn, "solemn and truculent in death, an idle chalice on his breast" (Si 18).

"INTENDED FOR A SPERMATOZOON WITH WINGS ADDED"

Every Joyce text mentions the Holy Spirit directly in various Joycean manners of reference: only *Dubliners* is almost totally devoid of direct reference, although replete with multiple manners of indirection. Joyce's directives vary from text to text, depending on tone and technique, subject matter and authorial innuendo. The range is an interesting one, best contrasted between an allusion that surfaces in *A Portrait* and a bit of dialogue almost lost in *Stephen Hero*:

He believed this all the more, and with trepidation, because of the divine gloom and silence wherein dwelt the unseen Paraclete, Whose symbols were a dove and a mighty wind, to sin against Whom was a sin beyond forgiveness, the eternal, mysterious secret Being to Whom, as God, the priests offered up mass once a year, robed in the scarlet of the tongues of fire.   (AP 149)

– . . . I feel a flame in my face. I feel a wind rush through me.
– "Like a mighty wind rushing," said Cranly.   (*SH* 142)

In the one instance Stephen is still close enough to his own spiritual identification with the Church to be able to state the case for the Holy Ghost without subjective intervention; in the other he has inadvertently, but immodestly, used the *language* of that spirituality for his own literary priesthood, only to have Cranly mock his self-centred intensity through immediate application of that same language, detached from its original centre. The component elements are present for Joyce's application in *Dubliners*: concrete symbolic factors and nebulous, ethereal qualities that can be woven together throughout a presumably naturalistic narrative for multiple purposes and possibilities by playing upon the same themes and sounding the familiar notes.

That something is wrong in the state of Catholic Ireland becomes apparent with the initial premiss, that the death of a Catholic cleric, inauspicious in itself and certainly worthy of solemnity and reverence, engenders instead gossip and suspicion in an atmosphere of depressed poverty. There is no intentional malice to the gossip, all the more symptomatic in the pathetic sympathy with which his own sister concedes that the priest's life had been "crossed", and the boy's aunt acknowledges that he was "a disappointed man" (Si 17). These are inadvertent phrases for a clergyman dedicated to the symbology of the Cross, someone more then merely a man in that he held an "appointed" position in the Church.

Eliza Flynn characterizes herself through ungrammatical constructions and trite phrases, an occasional malapropism ("the *Freeman's General*" – Si 16) and an unwitting pun (the priest's life as "crossed"). She confesses that her brother's death had dashed their hopes for a nostalgic visit to their childhood neighbourhood, a projected journey in "one of them new-fangled carriages . . . them with the rheumatic wheels" (Si 17). It is as understandable that Eliza Flynn should know very little about the recent innovations in automotive travel as that a disease like rheumatism would be close to her conscious thoughts. The missing portion of the word *pneumatics* suggests the absence of the Holy Ghost, the Greek *pneuma* designating wind, air or spirit. In the New Testament (Acts 2) "a sound came from heaven like the rush of a mighty wind" and those gathered on the day of Pentecost were "filled with the Holy Spirit". When Father Flynn died "You couldn't tell when the breath went out of him" (Si 15), and the carriage with the rheumatic wheels was to have been hired at Johnny Rush's. Behind the scenes lurks the figure of Father O'Rourke, who had told the Flynns about Johnny Rush's vehicles, had been instrumental in detecting the demented priest in the dark confessional, had taken care of such practical matters as funeral arrangements, announcements, insurance, and had been with the dying man on "Tuesday and annointed him and prepared him and all" (Si 15). This *eminence grise* has as typical an Irish name as the dead man, but it may have its deeper origins in the Hebrew word *ruach*, the word for the Spirit of God in the Old Testament, comparable to *pneuma* in the New.

The play of language that allows for speculation that Johnny Rush (despite his actually having been a Dublin garage proprietor) and Father O'Rourke contribute New and Old Testament nuances for the Holy Spirit can be substantiated within particularly appropriate contextual juxtapositions. "Rush" is certainly a common enough word, heightened only when Cranly gives it its allusive quality: its four subsequent appearances in *Dubliners* are generally inconspicuous, yet the circumstances under which Frank "rushed" toward the ship while Eveline remained clinging to the barrier "like a helpless animal" (Ev 41) – as an animal Eveline is without spirit – has its own heightened effect. Even more so does the phraseology of Gabriel Conroy's dinner speech:

> Here we are gathered together for a brief moment from the bustle and rush of our everyday routine. We are met here as friends, in the spirit of good-fellowship, as colleagues, also to a certain extent, in the true spirit of *camaraderie*, and as the guests of – what shall I call them? – the Three Graces of the Dublin musical world.   (De 204)

Rush, spirit, guests and the Trinity are felicitous accidents – if accidental – especially in a gathering which like the one on the day of Pentecost might have been visited by a rushing mighty wind.

Set within the celebration of the Christmas season, and most likely occurring on the night of or the evening before Epiphany, the dinner scene in "The Dead" may well parody the Pentecostal scene depicted in the Acts of the Apostles:

> And there appeared unto them cloven tongues like as of fire, and it sat upon each of them. And they were filled with the Holy Ghost, and began to speak with other tongues, as the spirit gave them utterance . . . every man heard them speak in his own language.

As a spirit intended as a momentous intrusion into a gathering, Gabriel is a disappointment. Rejecting quotations from Browning and even from Shakespeare for the common language of Tommy Moore, he is unable or unwilling to speak in tongues, assuming that the gathered would not be capable of hearing him in their own language. He has chosen specific words intended for Molly Ivors in particular, but she has absented herself from the dinner and his words fall on the wrong ears and prove meaningless. With no intention to amaze or confound, much less to infuse with a spiritual ebullience, Gabriel's language is blatantly cliché-ridden, and as a response to his address, all those assembled are invited to sing "in unison" the same familiar words, *"For they are jolly gay fellows . . . "* (De 205).

On an even more mundane level "Grace" concerns the loss of a bit of tongue. Tom Kernan's fall (from grace and into the pub lavatory) results in his having bitten off a minuscule piece of his tongue, making his speech rather unintelligible to those who attempt to lift him up: "I 'ery 'uch o'liged to you, sir" (Gr 152) – by comparison Mrs Hill managed to be totally unintelligible when she spoke in tongues ("Derevaun Seraun! Derevaun Seraun!" – Ev 40). Those who gather at Kernan's bedside have planned his spiritual redemption, although Mrs Kernan is somewhat sceptical, commenting (with tongue in cheek) that "Mr Kernan's tongue would not suffer by being shortened" (Gr 158). But the comforters, led by Martin Cunningham, resolutely keep the subject revolving around ecclesiastical matters, while Kernan remains unaware of the drift of their words, until they finally circle in on the proposed retreat. As the most eloquent of the group Cunningham comes closest to personifying the Holy Spirit, especially when he corroborates the doctrine of papal infallibility: "His deep raucous voice had thrilled them as it uttered the word of belief and submission" (Gr 170). (*Raucous* may be more than a descriptive word here, although it is as appropriate in its verbal setting as *O'Rourke* had been.) Just how distant the Kernans actually are from the *ruach* can be observed in the ecumenism of Mrs Kernan, whose "faith was bounded by her kitchen but, if she was put to it, she could believe also in the banshee and in the Holy Ghost" (Gr 158).

The return to grace of Tom Kernan is of course a "spiritual matter", as the devious Martin Cunningham asserts when Kernan colloquially inquires: "What's in the wind?" (Gr 162). This coupling of wind and spirit has its immediate recurrence: having ascertained that "some spiritual agencies were about to concern themselves on his behalf", Kernan becomes silent and suspicious, listening to the conversation "with an air of calm enmity" (Gr 163). The subject is the Jesuits, and having allowed himself to be taken to the retreat at the Jesuit church on Gardiner Street, he hears Father Purdon asking him to open "the books of his spiritual life" (Gr 174).

Semantic entities like air, wind, tongues, spirit profit by being offered in their various meanings, consistent patterns often emerging that sustain the impression that paralytic Dublin lacks the essentials of the Holy Spirit. In "After the Race" the spirit is decidedly secular, and even more commercial than Father Purdon would have intended: as they drive into Dublin the four young men are in fine "spirits" (Af 42), Villona is even in "excellent spirits", but Jimmy has difficulty guessing at the drift of their conversation and has to "shout back a suitable answer in the teeth of a high wind" (Af 44).

Lack of comprehension is diametrically inconsistent with the multinational gathering in the New Testament, even though the Frenchman, the French-Canadian and the Hungarian are speaking what is ironically Jimmy Doyle's language. Yet if the wind here intrudes to prevent understanding, a different sort of spirit works its magic on the gathering at dinner – and "their tongues had been loosened" (Af 46). The conviviality, however, is disturbed by political disputes where again they are at cross-purposes, and Jimmy in particular, under the influence of drink, becomes nationa-listic enough to offend the newcomer, the Englishman whose interesting name is Routh. Fresh air eventually is introduced to cool the argument, as is an innocuous toast with more good spirits: "The alert host at an opportunity lifted his glass to Humanity and, when

the toast had been drunk, he threw open a window significantly"
(Af 46).

"YOU WERE SPEAKING OF THE GASEOUS VERTEBRATE"

Dubliners is indeed a survey of the dispirited, as is best personified
in the mood of the less-than-gallant Lenehan. "Two Gallants" is set
in an August evening of "mild warm air" (Tw 49); he and Corley
stroll past the harpist playing "Silent, O Moyle" and the "notes of
the air throbbed deep and full" (Tw 54). By a deft manoeuvre Corley
detaches himself from Lenehan's company and as quickly unites
with the slavey instead, Lenehan getting only a whiff of her perfume
in departure, "the air heavily scented" (Tw 55). His pathetic attempt
to capture a momentary rapport with Corley, his doffing of his cap
to him, is met with only "a salute to the air" (Tw 56), as if Lenehan
did not exist but were merely a shade. Corley's absence weighs
heavily upon him as he passes the spot where the harpist had stood,
he too now also an absence: Lenehan's "gaiety seemed to forsake
him. . . . The air which the harpist had played began to control his
movements" (Tw 56). When he enters the working-class eatery
Lenehan tries to "belie his air of gentility" and is sensitive to "his
own poverty of purse and spirit" (Tw 57). A mere shade of what he
should be, a mockery of the proper bourgeois that is his class right
by birth but which he has allowed to flit away through indolence,
Lenehan is incomplete, a parasite that has lost its source in a
symbiotic relationship that has eluded him. His self-pitying
daydream of marriage and comfort follows upon his meagre meal,
which somewhat revives him, making him feel "less vanguished in
spirit" (Tw 58). Sycophant and sponge, drifter and dreamer, he is
unredeemed by these transitory revivals and persists as the
embodiment of the absence of true spirit – of any kind.

As is the Farrington of "Counterparts". Attempting to revive his
dispirited state with a great night of drinking, Farrington is
metaphorically a victim of his own tongue. His clever retort to his
employer, both his claim to momentary fame and the point of his
inevitable downfall, is the product of his tongue alone and not the
volitional product of his brain: "his tongue had found a felicitous
moment" (Co 91). Hardly a man of words, he had accidentally
found his tongue and succeeded in talking himself into more

trouble than he will ever be able to extricate himself from. The same tongue then had to form "an abject apology" and he later admonishes himself in private: "Could he not keep his tongue in his cheek?" (Tw 92). In public, however, he seeks to capitalize on his felicitous tongue, repeating his witticism for the edification of his cronies at Davy Byrne's. But nimbleness of tongue is not Farrington's forte, and although his tongue now dissembles to advantage, deleting the servile "sir" from the retort, he fails to carry it off. The sponge Higgins (a counterpart of Lenehan) arrives on the spot to retell Farrington's story to Farrington's discomfort, and it is Higgins who profits from free drinks. Farrington's suggestion of the Scotch House for further libations proves to be his undoing: it is there, with the bar "full of men and loud with the noise of tongues and glasses" (Co 94), that our Irish Goliath meets the English David, the artiste Weathers who defeats him in Indian armwrestling. (The "noise of tongues" in "Counterparts" parallels the situation in "The Dead", where Gabriel, smarting from the abuse he feels Molly Ivors has subjected him to, retreats to a "remote corner" where Mrs Malins in babbling away: "While her tongue rambled on Gabriel tried to banish from his mind all memory of the unpleasant incident with Miss Ivors" – De 190.)

"Air" as music is present not only in "Two Gallants", where associations with the national spirit and its downfallen state persist, but importantly in "Eveline" and "The Dead". In the former it is a melody played by a street organ as Eveline prepares to leave Dublin, and she remembers it as the same air played by an Italian organ grinder on the evening in which her mother departed this life. It is a foreign air, and Mr Hill curses the "damned Italians" who have emigrated to Ireland, but although he fails to understand these foreigners, neither does he nor Eveline understand Mrs Hill's dying words, As the spirit leaves her she speaks in tongues ("Derevaun Seraun!" – Ev 40), probably in the tongue of her Irish forebears, although it passes as insane gibberish, uncomprehended in a land that has been deprived of its national spirit. (Air of course is the central metaphor of the story. Concerned with its corruption as dust throughout the house, Eveline hopes to exchange it for the good air of "Buenos Ayres". The air that evolves into music would normally be present in a harmonium, often used for hymn music, but at the Hills' house the harmonium is broken.)

In the latter story, "The Dead", music is central to the social occasion, and both air as wind and air as melody contain references to the world of spirit. The opening scene depicts the arrivals at the festivities: the hall-door bell is "wheezy" as each "guest" is admitted (De 175), etymologically setting up the interplay between host and ghost, guest and ghastly, that persists throughout the story. Gabriel's entrance in particular is marked by the "cold fragrant air from out-of-doors" (De 177), and throughout the evening he yearns for the outdoors ("The air was pure there" – De 202), but spends his time in the hot atmosphere of the Morkans' house "airing his superior education" (De 179). For many at the gathering, however, the cold air outside is mistrusted: "the east wind blowing in" had caused Gretta to catch cold the year before (De 180), and Bartell D'Arcy is warned against the danger to his throat from "the night air" (De 211). By contrast the deathlike environment of Mount Melleray, where the monks sleep in their coffins and the burghers of Dublin take the cure, is praised: "how bracing the air was down there" (De 200). A significant indication of musical air as spirit occurs when Aunt Julia sings the inappropriate "Arrayed for the Bridal": "Her voice, strong and clear in tone, attacked with great spirit the runs which embellish the air and though she sang very rapidly she did not miss even the smallest of grace notes" (De 193). This linkage of air/spirit/grace points toward Gretta's mystical experience, when the hoarse singer unconsciously succeeds in transfixing her with "The Lass of Aughrim". The mystified Gabriel is trying "to catch the air that the voice was singing and gazing up at his wife. There was grace and mystery in her attitude" (De 210).

"Mystery" is a key word in *Dubliners*, particularly in the early stories devoted to a young boy's emerging awareness of certain "mysteries". Echoed as it is in "The Dead", religious mystery held in the hands of the initiate comes full circle from the boy's thwarted aspirations in "The Sisters". The child who was in awe of "how complex and mysterious were certain institutions of the Church" (Si 13) loses whatever potential he had assumed when Father Flynn is demoted and degraded (*demystified*) by the sisters' gossip. The boy's counterpart in "An Encounter" shares a "spirit of unruliness" with his classmates (En 20), and his encounter with the pederast, a degraded surrogate for Father Flynn, is shrouded in mystery for him. The old man speaks "mysteriously" (En 26), and his extolling of flagellation is presented as "unfolding some elaborate mystery", the auditor sensing that he is being led "through the mystery" by the hypnotic voice (En 27). Subsequent "mysteries" in *Dubliners* include the missing plumcake in "Clay" and Father Keon's means of earning a living in "Ivy Day", the theme of the displaced priest leading directly from the Father Butler whose possible presence at the Pigeon House is categorically dismissed, and the priest in "Eveline" whose yellowing photograph surmounts the broken harmonium, to Gabriel Conroy's brother. If Gabriel appears as an adult extension of the boy in "The Sisters", his secular role and attitudes are all the more understandable, and it is doubly ironic that his brother (aptly named Constantine) is a priest who is not present or even discussed at the Christmastime family gathering, a ghost by absence.

The absence of such clerics as Father Conroy, through death or departure or misplacement or even non-placement (out of sight and therefore out of mind), compounds the lack of the spiritual essence. Since the Holy Ghost personifies "mystery of love", "spirit of Grace" and "the unity of God and Christ", the cluster of such phrases throughout *Dubliners* takes definite shape. Each story moves from a promise or possibility of spiritual presence to a nadir of absence, usually through the symbolic positioning of one or both of the elements of air or fire (mighty rushing wind, tongues of fire). Whereas "Araby" and "Eveline" begin with musty and dusty air respectively, and the hopes of release in Araby and Buenos Ayres prove shortlived, other tales reverse the opening significance of air. "After the Race", for example, not only begins in a high wind but also with an "unmistakable air of wealth" (Af 45), which Jimmy Doyle hopes to duplicate, but dissipates instead. The Sunday morning of "The Boarding House" is ushered in with a "fresh breeze blowing" (Bo 63), but Doran's flashback focuses on the eventful night when Polly's candle was "blown out by a gust" and he allowed himself to be seduced by her dress, her fingers and her "breath" (Bo 67). The Little Chandler who walks to his rendezvous with Gallaher finds that the air had grown sharp" (Li 71), but is temporarily intrigued by his friend's "travelled air" (Li 70) and walks resolutely toward disappointment. His attempt to recoup his lost self-esteem leads him to reading Byron's juvenilia (*"Hushed are the winds and still the evening gloom, / Not e'en a Zephyr wanders through the grove"* – Li 83), but the wailing of his child disturbs his retreat from mundane reality. And his frightening the baby causes it to lose "its breath for four or five seconds" (Li 84).

"ROBED IN THE SCARLET OF THE TONGUES OF FIRE"

The element of fire takes various forms in Dubliners, from candles and gas to grates and furnaces. Critics who decry symbol-hunting in so "straightforward" a text as this volume of short stories have been quick to dismiss concentrated critical focus on the atmospheric conditions in the committee room on Ivy Day, where as much attention is given to the ineffective fire in the grate as to the memory of Parnell. The pitiful fire in the cold room suggests a scene in Hell, a Dantean Hell that is apt for the roomful of mild turncoats, frauds, malcontents and hypocrites; the pathetic fire that offers neither warmth nor light serves as a recurring reminder of a congregation devoid of spiritual substance. Similar occurrences of the "failed" hearth appear as early as "The Sisters", where the boy's disillusionment began with the innuendoes of Old Cotter, who "spat rudely into the grate" (Si 10), and the elaboration of these innuendoes by Eliza Flynn as she "gazed into the empty grate" (Si 17). For the boy in "Araby" disillusionment also began with the intrusion of an adult visitor ("I found Mrs Mercer sitting at the fire" – Ar 33), and culminated with his being plunged into darkness and despair: "I heard a voice call from one end of the gallery that the light was out. The upper part of the hall was now completely dark" (Ar 35).

The loss of light that concludes "Araby" – the heavens in darkness – has its reverberations in several other stories, in each case highlighting the dejection and degradation that pervades in the absence of the Holy Spirit. When dawn breaks for Jimmy Doyle, it is a "shaft of grey light" (Af 48); when Corley displays the spoils obtained from his victimization of the slavey it is "with a grave gesture he extended a hand towards the light" (Tw 60); and when Chandler is disgraced in the eyes of his angry wife "his cheeks suffused with shame and he stood back out of the lamplight" (Li 85). Turning one's back on the light has its ecclesiastic significance in "Grace", where the light before the altar is seen as a "distant speck of red light" (Gr 172) and Father Purdon takes his text from the parable of the unjust steward: "*For the children of his world are wiser in their generation than the children of light*" (Gr 173).

The most dramatic presentation of the light that failed is observed in "Counterparts". Farrington's day has been a disaster, but it becomes apparent to him only as the day diminishes and his work has no chance of being completed, dramatized by his realization that "evening was falling and in a few minutes they would be lighting the gas" (Co 88). Deluding himself into thinking that this would facilitate his work, he none the less sneaks off for a drink, now aware that "Darkness, accompanied by a thick fog, was gaining upon the dusk of February and the lamps in Eustace Street had been lit." Like the young lover yearning for the mysteries of Araby, Farrington anticipates evening and "longed to spend it in the bars, drinking with his friends amid the glare of gas and the clatter of glasses" (Co 89). But the evening proves as much a disaster as the day, and night finds him at home, a domain now as hostile as the office, and "he found the kitchen empty and the kitchen fire nearly out", angrily ordering his son to "Light the lamp" (Co 97). In a rage he beats the boy, accompanying the violence with a three-part incantation: "You let the fire out! . . . I'll teach you to let the fire out! . . . Now, you'll let the fire out the next time!" (Co 98). Young Tom attempts to parry the Apocalyptic threat of "Fire the next time" with an offer to say a *Hail Mary* for his father, inadvertently corroborating the religious pattern.

In echo of the invocation of the Blessed Virgin, the opening of the next story introduces Maria, identified as a "veritable peace-maker" (Cl 99). She is observed at her kitchen fire ("nice and bright"), and anticipates leaving it on a mission of kindness to children – her own surrogate child and his children. Fire seems to be Maria's totem, in keeping with the Irish celebration of the fire festival of Samhain on that night, with games and fortune-telling predicting marriages and death: at the Donnelly home she stays close to the grate, Joe Donnelly having "made her sit down by the fire" (Cl 104): her arrival elicits a demotic translation of young Tom's *Ave Maria*: "Everybody said: *O, here's Maria!*" (Cl 103). It is only when she ventures away from the fire to the divination saucers and the piano that Maria unconsciously discloses the despair of her life, her lost hopes, her naive secret yearnings, her morbid fate.

By contrast, the bachelor counterpart of this reluctant spinster is Mr Duffy, a man for whom all lights seem to fail. His political enthusiasms wane in the meeting room of the Irish Socialist Party, "a garret lit by an inefficient oil-lamp" (Pa 110–11), and his tenuous relationship with Mrs Sinico is conducted in her cottage, where "Many times she allowed the dark to fall upon them, refraining from lighting the lamp" (Pa 111). As he sits in his room re-reading the newspaper account of her sordid death, "the light failed and his memory began to wander" as he senses the ghost of Emily Sinico touching his hand (Pa 116). But Duffy soon realizes that he is being denied even the companionship of such a ghost and will remain totally alone. His carefully chosen residence is across from a "disused distillery" (Pa 107) – where spirits are no longer made – and now he gazes out the window at that "empty distillery and from time to time a light appeared in some house on the Lucan road" (Pa 115). Mrs Sinico had taken to drinking and was "in the habit of going out at night to buy spirits" (Pa 115).

It is "Ivy Day", however, that has the major concentration of fire references, although nothing can gainsay the accuracy of the verisimilitudinistic function of the fireplace in the narrative, nor the atmospheric impression that follows logically from the repeated observations of its persistent inadequacy. Yet the 22 direct allusions to it could well be considered ancillary if they did not lead into the resolution of the narrative. Joe Hynes's reading of "The Death of Parnell" sums up the Parnellite ideals and delusions, illuminating the banalities and hopelessness of the latter-day disciples assembled in the room. Hynes is coaxed into reading it by Mat O'Connor with the demand, "Fire away, Joe" (Iv 133), and the poem (like Byron's in "A Little Cloud" and Bunn's lyrics in "Clay") contains the root language of the pathetic condition. Parnell's death is equated with the death of Ireland's aspirations, since *"Erin's hopes and Erin's dream / Perish upon her monarch's pyre"* (Iv 134). The fire than consumes, however, may also be the fire of resurrection (this particular Ivy Day is the eleventh anniversary of Parnell's death, the Kabalistic indicator for regeneration), and Hynes's verses contain that hope:

> *his spirit may*
> *Rise, like the Phoenix from the flames,*
> *When breaks the dawning of the day.*
> (Iv 135)

Yet in the resulting dénouement, no further mention is made of the pale fire in the room, although the bottle on the hob emits its belated and ignored *Pok!* (Iv 135), the gases having expanded sufficiently to eject the cork.

Candles and candlelight provide another category and even more precise conjuring up of "tongues of fire". As mere secular items of lighting in a Dublin not yet subject to extensive electrification, they often have extended importance within the narrational frame: the candle that Polly requests Bob Doran relight for her, the candles that are lit in the committee room so that by contrast "the fire lost all its cheerful colour" (Iv 120), the possible play on the etymology of Chandler's name, and the porter's candle at the Gresham Hotel that Gabriel rejects. Gabriel seems indifferent to any sexual connotations attached to candles, although Polly could be credited with an awareness of the suggestiveness of hers, and his elaborate refusal of the old man's "guttering candle"(also referred to as "his unstable candle" – De 215) assumes almost comic proportions. That Gretta's thoughts in the hotel room are otherwise engaged results in Gabriel's acknowledgement that "the dull fires of his lust began to glow angrily in his veins" (De 219), whereas earlier he had felt that "a keen pang of lust" was brought about by a "kindling again of so many memories, the first touch of her body, musical and strange and perfumed" (De 215). The Gresham Hotel already has electricity, although it is not functioning, but rather than the candle, Gabriel prefers the light "from the street", soon after described as a "ghostly light from the street lamp" (De 216). Michael Furey, who now makes his belated entrance into Gabriel's consciousness, is revealed as having been "a boy in the gasworks" (De 219).

The death of the "boy in the gasworks" returns us full circle to the funereal candles that dominate the opening story of *Dubliners*, where a boy regards them as revelatory beacons that will announce the death of Father Flynn: "If he was dead, I thought, I would see the reflection of candles on the darkened blind for I knew that two candles must be set at the head of a corpse" (Si 9). Yet the signal fails: either the candles are not visible to him or he does not pass the house on the night of the actual death. Instead, the news is conveyed by a despised messenger sitting by the fire and puffing on his pipe, a usurper in the boy's house. When the ceremonial visit is made to the Flynns, the windows do not reveal the candles but only reflect a cloudy sunset, one more deflection from the possibility of a glimpse of the true flame. Once inside, the boy determines that the sunset diminishes the power of the candles, which "looked like pale thin flames" (Si 14), yet the candles are there, having been supplied by Father O'Rourke, "two candlesticks out of the chapel" (Si 16). Poor competition for even a cloudy crepuscular sky, the ecclesiastical candles at least have no competition from the hearth, for although a fire is set in the boy's

house, none is lighted at the poorer Flynns' – twice we are directed
to the "empty fireplace" and the "empty grate" (Si 15, 17).

The emphasis on specifically religious candles is heaviest in
"Grace", although they have been adumbrated by an incident in the
committee room where Mr Henchy dutifully lights Father Keon's
way out, despite the priest's polite protests. The implication seems
to be that the "black sheep" priest, now redirected to Tierney's
Black Eagle pub, can see in the dark:

> Mr. Henchy, seizing one of the candlesticks, went to the door to
> light him downstairs.
> – O, don't trouble, I beg!
> – No, but the stairs is so dark.
> – No, no, I can see. . . . Thank you, indeed.
> – Are you right now?
> – All right, thanks. . . . Thanks.
> Mr Henchy returned with the candlestick and put it on the table.
>   (Iv 126)

This touch of allegiance to the clergy does not prevent Henchy's
participation in the gossip behind the back of the "unfortunate
man", much like the gossip of the sisters of the departed Father
Flynn.

The comic climax of "Grace" occurs when Tom Kernan, suavely
manoeuvred into agreeing to participate in the religious retreat,
makes his "Protestant" objections to the carrying of a candle.
Martin Cunningham had somewhat overplayed his hand by
confidently asserting, "All we have to do . . . is to stand up with
lighted candles in our hands and renew our baptismal vows", and
M'Coy is even heavier-handed in his exclamations of "O, don't
forget the candle, Tom . . . whatever you do." Backsliding Kernan
can then make his belated stand, four times insisting, "No candles!"
(Gr 171–2). That his last stand is merely a gesture becomes apparent
in the final scene where he is present at the Jesuit church, although
the impact of his "gesture" should not be overlooked. His refusal is
made "sensibly", at least at first (Gr 171), but as he becomes
overheated on the subject, the descriptive adverb shifts to
"obdurately" (Gr 172). Kernan is none the less "conscious of having
created an effect on his audience", and the reiterated strictures
against candles gives him a chance to save face to a certain extent,
especially as he delights in scoring the religious ceremony as

"magic-lantern business" (Gr 171). Indeed, the candles are meant to "reflect" the Holy Spirit, and categorizing them as magic-lantern business presupposes a certain sleight of hand, as well as an occupational function. The "farcical gravity" of Kernan's gestures (Gr 171) provides the oxymoron that highlights the basic contradiction, and his acceptance-with-reservations parallels the diminished religiosity of the *businessmen's* retreat at the Gardiner Street church. Kernan barring the candles corresponds to Gabriel's similar gesture, as the one expresses his religious ambivalence and the other his confused sexual intentions. (It should be noted that the scene in the church only concerns itself with the preliminary seating and kneeling of the congregation, and the beginning of the sermon, without arriving at the ceremony of the candles.)

A Dublin devoid of spirituality unfolds in Joyce's *Dubliners* through ironic juxtapositions, oblique inferences and deft comic wordplay, anticipating the techniques of *Ulysses* and the Dublin depicted there. The Kernan scene builds from the sensible to the obdurate, from Kernan's serious protest against ceremonial excess to the excessive absurdity of his inflated gesturing, as the comic eventually comes into play. Although it may still be a long step to Buck Mulligan's designation of the Holy Ghost as "the gaseous vertebrate" (SC 487), the stage is set in Dubliners for just such irreverences, where "gas" (fire plus air) plays itself out in several of the stories, with the major concentration in "The Dead". Farrington sets serious stock in his preference for the gaslit evenings, as does the boy in "Araby", finally released to make his journey to the bazaar, as he associates the sight of the streets "glaring with gas" with the purpose of that journey (Ar 34). These tenuous associations of gas with wish-fulfilment are serious in tone, yet the repetitious references to pathetic Michael Furey as "in the gasworks" allies pathos with comedy (Gretta's comments remain neutral, but the "translation" by Gabriel reveals little sympathy", especially since the derided Mr Browne is facetiously described by Aunt Kate as having been "laid on here like the gas" (De 206).

"QUI VOUS A MIS DANS CETTE FICHUE POSITION?"

A third representation of the Holy Spirit, that of the Dove, is the least prevalent in *Dubliners*, yet its handful of instances call attention to themselves, especially as they are at times intricately coupled with fire and gas. Comic wordplay, for example, suggests that the Holy Dove has its residence in the Pigeon House in "An Encounter", and like the bazaar for the boy in "Araby" and the various public houses for Farrington, the Pigeon House looms large as the destination of the truants: whether by their own dalliance or by misjudging the distance, they fail to attain it, nor is there any reason to suppose that they would not have found it as disappointing as the Araby Bazaar and the pubs. That Father Butler has his "place" in the classroom, and hardly likely to be at the Pigeon House instead, makes good sense when explained ("sensibly") by Mahony (En 21), yet Leo Dillon had somehow imagined the priest's presence there, probably more out of apprehensiveness at the possibility of their being caught there by their feared schoolmaster than any subliminal association of Christianity and the Pigeon House. By the turn of the century the building in Ringsend that had been built by a man named Pidgeon was already in use as an electrical power plant, and by accident of misspelling it serves better for the kind of punned association that Stephen makes in *Ulysses* with the Holy Dove. The family connection of course exists between pigeons and doves, but to reduce the rarified dove to the commonness of pigeons is only the first step toward Stephen's blasphemy.

On the road to the Pigeon House the boys give up short of their announced goal, probably because the narrator is so often deflected by his interest in ships and sailors, while his cohort prefers chasing cats and ragged urchins, exhausting themselves to the extent that they find that they are stranded in the domain of the "queer old josser" rather than that of the Holy Dove. Significant in considering the causes of the failed mission is the surprising news that Mahony has brought along a slingshot, in order to "have some gas with the birds", a phrase that the narrator explains in terms of Mahony's frequent use of slang, along with references to Father Butler as "Bunsen Burner" (En 22). With two deft strokes the associations are comically assembled of gas, fire and bird, without interfering with the less facetious concern that the House of the Holy Dove is without its Catholic priest and out-of-reach for these pupils of a Catholic school.

It is in "The Dead" that many of these birds come home to roost, and the comic dimensions of symbolic materials become even more expansive. The aviary world provides the narrative with parodic distortions of language, innocuous enough in their isolated places but forming a pattern when they flock together. Molly Ivors is innocently responsible for introducing a colloquialism that sets the motif into play: "I have a crow to pluck with you", she says (De 187). Gabriel is discomfited by her fervent nationalism, and his indifference to her nationalist ideals is apparent in his preference for cycling vacations on the Continent over a patriotic voyage to the West of Ireland. His sojourns out of the country ironically ally him with those who had been exiled after the Battle of the Boyne, but it is Molly who flees from the dinner scene and Gabriel who is assigned to carving the "fat brown goose" (actually volunteering to "carve a flock of geese, if necessary" – De 196). (Stephen Dedalus took pleasure in labelling the fervently nationalist Davin as "my little tame goose" – AP 201.) The brown goose has its echo in the name of the token Protestant present at the festivities, Mr Browne, and when Aunt Julia worries that the pudding may not be brown enough, he quips, "I hope . . . that I'm brown enough for you because, you know, I'm all brown" (De 200). It is Browne who will later direct the cab driver to "Make like a bird for Trinity College" (De 209).

Such colloquial expressions are certainly unobtrusive in context because of their apt placement in the dialogue, but the overall motif that unites them is the loss of the spiritual centre of a self-determined and Catholic Ireland. Browne as a Protestant is a subtly intrusive element (balancing the absence of Father Conroy), but the one newcomer to the fold is the tenor Bartell D'Arcy, who, although he insists that he is unable to sing, disturbs Gabriel's precarious equilibrium by singing the song from the West of Ireland that sets off Gretta's nostalgia. Afterward, however, D'Arcy still protests that he is "as hoarse as a crow" (De 211).

The Dublin of *Dubliners* is impregnated with musty indoor air and treacherous night air outside, but no gale, the symbol of the strength of the Holy Spirit, blows through. Hoarse crows and roasted geese replace the Dove whose House is unattained. Tongues prattle in pubs but no communion of voices resounds to unite the disparate elements of the nation. Fires burn without giving warmth or light and candles are rejected. Several vignettes serve to focus on the spiritless dilemma: the disconsolate Gabriel recalls the fervour of his "secret life" with Gretta when "Birds were twittering in the ivy", and at a glass-blower's he noticed Gretta's face "fragrant in the cold air", when she called out to the man at the furnace, "Is the fire hot, sir?" (De 213). Eveline Hill also has a happy memory: when she was sick and her father was nice to her, "he had read her out a ghost story and made toast for her at the fire" (Ev 39), in past days when the spirit was still willing. And most important is that back garden inherited from the dead priest by the boy in "Araby": it combines the totem of the knowledge of Good and Evil and the remnant of the disused Holy Spirit: "The wild garden behind the house contained a central apple-tree and a few straggling bushes under one of which I found the late tenant's rusty bicycle-pump" (Ar 29). The bicycle pump joins the rheumatic wheels and broken harmonium and the Pigeon House and Buenos Ayres and Bunsen Burner as the tangible clues to the great disappearance that is dissected throughout Joyce's *Dubliners*.

4
Pounds/Shillings/Pence: The Economics in the Tales

"Luncheon interval. A sixpenny at Rowe's? Must look up that ad in the national library. An eightpenny in the Burton. Better. On my way."

(Le 368–70)

"1 *Lunch* $0 - 0 - 7$"

(It 1464)

"A TIME HAS A TENSE . . . AT THE PLACE AND PERIOD"

The Dubliners of *Dubliners* occupy fifteen designated areas of that city, a territorial separation that allows for just enough overlappings to attest to the "unity" of Dublin more than to the unity of the text. Unlike the citizens of *Ulysses* that many of them will eventually become, they have almost no points of contact with each other, and is not until late in the process that a journalist for the *Freeman* named Hendrick, who was scheduled to review the *Eire Abu* concert in "A Mother", turns up at the businessmen's retreat in "Grace", while Kathleen Kearney, who had figured so prominently in "A Mother", is mentioned by Molly Ivors in "The Dead". Almost all of the characters in the fifteen tales are (temporarily) confined within the space of their individual narratives. Whereas *Ulysses* will later reprise some of them, they are essentially "fictional" characters who displace the real people of James Joyce's Dublin for the purpose of the fiction. Also in sharp contradistinction there is no attempt to introduce real and fictional people to each other (like J. C. Doyle and Molly Bloom on the concert stage, Myler Keogh and Percy Bennett in the boxing ring, George Russell and Stephen

84

Dedalus in the National Library). At least one known personage, however, the English Jesuit Father Bernard Vaughan, mentioned by his actual name in *Ulysses*, is portrayed in *Dubliners* by a fictional surrogate, Father Purdon.

Another aspect of reality, on the other hand, is already prefigured in the earlier book, the use of actual place names that give Joyce's Dublin its topographical verisimilitude, with an emphasis on the names of certain business establishments of Joyce's day: Pim's, the Stores, Johnny Rush's, Terry Kelly's – and particularly a selection of pubs and bookdealers (O'Neill's, Davy Byrne's, the Scotch House, Mulligan's of Poolbeg Street, Michael Hickey's, George Webb's, Edward Massey's). These real concerns casually co-exist in *Dubliners* with "invented" establishments, especially when the author considered diplomacy the better part of validity: Crosbie and Alleyne's, the *Eire Abu* Society, the Liffey Loan Bank, the Black Eagle, old Mr Leonard's wine business. A fine example of Joyce's handling of the familiar in terms of the quasi-fictional is the reference to Corless's, the restaurant where (in "A Little Cloud") Chandler arranges to meet Gallaher, and obviously very much Gallaher's home turf: the restaurant was The Burlington and its proprietor was Thomas Corless. And the bartender on that particular evening, whom Gallaher cavalierly calls "garçon" and "François" (Li 74, 78), probably answered more often to a real local name like Frank or Francis.

There is no attempt in *Dubliners* to present a firm anchor in time to parallel the fixity of place, nothing comparable to the Thursday, 16 June 1904 of *Ulysses*, so that even an attempt to read the succession of stories sequentially necessarily falls apart. There are surprisingly few time frames in any of the stores, merely an overall impression that they cluster at the turn of the twentieth century, although mostly in the 1890s, and eventually abut closely to the Ulyssean year of Joyce's departure from Dublin. Vagueness of time is especially functional in the first three stories: if we are tempted to assume that the boy in "The Sisters", "An Encounter" and "Araby" is the same person throughout, then he must be allowed to mature over several years, without the span of his age or the specifics of his age ever indicated. Directional signals of historical time are generally more apparent in the later stories, those that specify a "time present" for the events, based on a combination of explicit data within the frame of the story and verifiable events implicit in Irish history. "Ivy Day in the Committee Room" depends on a definite occasion and consequently a definite date, 6 October 1902, but only to those aware that Charles Stewart Parnell died on that day eleven years earlier. It seems safely conjectural that "The Dead" is set on 5–6 January (Twelfth Night/the Feast of the Epiphany), probably just after the London sensation in 1903 of Enrico Caruso, as would be well known to the dinner guests at the Morkans, but these dates are left without irrefutable substantiation on just the basis of internal evidence.

At the earlier end of the spectrum is the date of the Araby Bazaar in May 1894, when Joyce himself was twelve years old – an age the reader may or may not be willing to assign to the protagonist of "Araby". Reluctance to do so may derive from the existence of a blatantly recorded date at the outset, that of the death of Father Flynn in "The Sisters": "July 1st, 1895" (Si 12). (If fictional and historical dating were allowed to co-exist, the boy would find himself regressing in age from "The Sisters" to "Araby", an unlikely scenario.) "The Sisters" underwent several rewritings along the way to inclusion in *Dubliners*, and the designation for Flynn's demise changed during the various versions until it arrived at the specifics of the age 65 in the year 1895, perhaps so that the priest's probable date of conception would be in 1829, the year of Catholic Emancipation.

Another kind of time-barometer concentrates on Dublin's status as a British city, not just in the detailed reminders planted throughout the stories (and especially laden in "Two Gallants"), but in those that the accidents of time and the dominance of history have since made apparent. For Joyce's purposes it was apt that Father Flynn, who had been born in Irishtown, should end his days of dissatisfaction living in Great Britain Street, and that Corley and Lenehan should be tracked in their wanderings from Rutland Square: both the street and the square have since been renamed for Charles Stewart Parnell. Maria alights from her tram at Nelson's Pillar, and although that totem of British imperial power remained in place for many decades into the Irish Free State and the Republic, it too is now an anachronism best "reconstructed" from the works of James Joyce. The statue of King Billy (William of Orange to his loyal subjects), the focus of Gabriel Conroy's anecdote about his grandfather's horse, did not last nearly as long as that of Nelson. Kingsbridge Station, from which James Duffy hears a train emerging, has been renamed, as has the Kingstown Station where Jimmy Doyle and his party emerge to board the yacht. The demise of the position of English royalty in Ireland played havoc with the Royal University, where Gabriel took his degree, and the Theatre Royal, where the opera company performed to the delight of some of those assembled at the Morkans' dinner table. And Mr Duggan, the operatic bass, once sang the role of "the king in the opera of *Maritana* at the Queen's Theatre" (MO 142).

"COMMERCIAL MEN ENGAGED IN SEDENTARY OCCUPATIONS"

The professional common denominator in *Dubliners* is that of the office clerk (Farrington, Chandler, Duffy, Doran, Donnelly – at various levels), the white-collar worker with eminent claims of respectability but often with only a tenuous hold on economic solvency. James Duffy's bank job is the most prestigious and seems the most secure, while Farrington is obviously unsuited for sedentary office work and in imminent danger of being booted out. His grasp on class privilege is slipping, yet as he steals away from his work for a quick drink, his ploy is to secrete a cap in his pocket: the chief clerk, seeing Farrington's hat still on the rack, is expected to assume that he is still in the building, for he would hardly risk a loss of class identity by appearing on the street without suitable head-covering. With a fairly sizable family to support Farrington can least afford to lose his job; Duffy, on the other hand, has only himself to provide for and a much more adequate salary with which to do it. Physically and temperamentally unsuited to a confining office and better equipped for manual labor, Farrington must deem class status as sufficiently important to resort to desperate acts of subterfuge.

Even if this particular clerk deserves the sack for inefficiency (much less insubordination), Thomas Chandler does not: there is every reason to believe that he is competent in his office (although a would-be poet on occasion, he does not yet seem to consider himself superior to his mode of employment), and in a fair world his job would be secure. Whereas there is no indication in "A Little Cloud" that he is in any danger of losing that job, there is a hint in "Counterparts" that he may indeed be vulnerable. Farrington recalls that someone known as "little Peake" was "hounded" out of his job for no reason other than "to make room for [the boss's] nephew" (Co 92) – what job security then for "little Chandler"? Both Farrington and Chandler, at opposite ends of the equation in almost every way, none the less offend against the sanctity of their bourgeois positions: the strong-man with a reputation to uphold and the poet with a reputation to establish both fail to conform completely to type. The experiences at Corless's with Gallaher and back at home with his wife may have the effect of convincing little Chandler to tread carefully and keep his urge to break out of his bounds well hidden. "A Little Cloud" may serve as a cautionary tale for its protagonist, but there is no way of learning how little Chandler reads the tale.

When Eveline Hill momentarily chooses to give up her demeaning job in the Stores (salary: seven shillings a week), she realizes that she will be quickly replaced, but a need for security and an overpowering sense of responsibility conspired to paralyse her in the act of escape. Other Dubliners, particularly men, may have managed to shake off bourgeois burdens and opt for lives of precarious freedom: John Corley is perfecting his talents as a gigolo of sorts, while his crony Lenehan cadges drinks by wobbly wit and threadbare subterfuge:

> Most people considered Lenehan a leech but, in spite of this reputation, his adroitness and eloquence had always prevented his friends from forming any general policy against him. He had a brave manner of coming up to a party of them in a bar and of holding himself nimbly at the borders of the company until he was included in a round. He was a sporting vagrant armed with a vast stock of stories, limericks and riddles.   (Tw 50)

"Two Gallants" tracks the ascendant line of Corley's progress toward the attainment of a "small gold coin" (Tw 60), apparently a half-sovereign (more than Eveline earns in a week in the Stores), while Lenehan's arc, on the other hand, is correspondingly descending. He finds himself tired and hungry, and condescends to eat a plate of peas in a "poor-looking shop" on a "dark quiet street" off Rutland Square, where the other customers, "two work-girls and a mechanic" (Tw 57), eye him with suspicion.

In his venture into the eatery, Lenehan has crossed over a line more decisive than just an avoidance of a sedentary occupation, and in order to find acceptance in so proletarian an ambience he attempts to "belie his air of gentility" (Tw 57) by assuming crass table manners. But having stepped out of his class territory, very much like Eveline stepping out of her role as a moral woman of her class, Lenehan seems to realize how insecure he is without his class identity, and in a moment of weakness even yearns for the perks of bourgeois respectability:

> He was tired of knocking about, of pulling the devil by the tail, of shifts and intrigues. He would be thirty-one in November. Would he never get a good job? He thought how pleasant it would be to have a warm fire to sit by and a good dinner to sit down to. . . . He might yet be able to settle down in some snug corner and live happily if he could only come across some good simple-minded girl with a little of the ready.   (Tw 57–8)

The transition from entertaining the notion of actually taking on a job to preferring to exploit a pliable female results from his having temporarily satisfied his hunger. He has quickly shifted from a possible but unlikely option to a far more remote, even impossible, option, and in effect is still under the spell of Corley's power to manipulate women and thus avoid gainful employment, assuming, of course, that suitable jobs were actually available.

With his experiences in the ways of the world Farrington might well be able to advise reform-minded Lenehan on the pitfalls of twilit daydreaming: that husbands may relapse into habitual pub-crawling instead of heading home to the warm fire and good dinner; that good simple-minded girls may evolve into wives who retreat to the chapel of an evening; that the good dinner may have to be reheated by an inefficient child who has let the warm fire die out. (But Farrington may not have been as calculating in his choice of a pliable wife, and the airtight compartments of the *Dubliners* tales never allow the participants to learn from each other's experiences – much less their own.) Farrington could hardly be expected to discern the shifts in Lenehan's speculations from real concern to an exalted variation of his usual "shifts and intrigues" (Two 50), occasioned by the gratification from a plate of peas (in "Ivy Day" a bottle of stout, with the same subtlety of elision, was all that was needed to alter Mr Henchy's mistrust of Joe Hynes).

For the duration of the story Lenehan remains an incorrigible "gallant", a segment of the middle class that views itself as kicking over the traces but in actuality is being summarily dumped in order to make room for those who embody the mores of the class more adequately. The bourgeois pie can be cut into larger slices if fewer claimants insist on their share, so the unspoken rule has been to allow various members to fall quietly away, to move into a grey area of their own. In *Ulysses* both gallants return for an ironic encore: Corley's ascent has proved short-lived, and late at night he is discovered derelict and alone, friendless, homeless, penniless, panhandling from Stephen Dedalus, while Lenehan has temporarily persevered (his association with racing tissues has strengthened), still living by his wits. Yet his newfound status may be on the wane as well: his touting of Sceptre for the Gold Cup has backfired with the win by Throwaway, earning him the enmity of so important a swell as Blazes Boylan. Corley should have retained the advantage of his family connections (he is "the son of an inspector of police" – Tw 51), but his descent into begging seems to indicate that he has been disinherited by the father he physically resembles, cast into the grey area by his own family.

"A PENNY SAVED"

Joyce operates not only as a chronicler of his class but also as its severest critic, so that every time-revered precept of the middle class is scrutinized and dismantled in *Dubliners*: that they are hardworking, thrifty, honest, religious and moral, temperate, serious and secure. Those who succeed best profit from the hard work of others or finagle lucrative contacts for themselves (whatever their sense of personal honesty, it does not prevent them from entering into shady business practices), and their piety is manipulated to consolidate social and economic advantage and control. Mr Alleyne can play the suave gallant with Miss Delacour while the Farringtons are busy copying out the correspondence under the watchful eye of the chief clerk. Mrs Mooney can feel assured that Bob Doran will do the right thing and marry her daughter since Doran is aware that any scandal will bring down upon him the wrath of his employer, the Catholic wine merchant, Mr Leonard. Mr Fitzpatrick can blithely shortchange Kathleen Kearney, confident that he has only the girl and her mother to deal with (Mr Kearney has been abstracted out of the situation). And Mr Duffy, who apparently does his job well as a cashier in a private bank, has dissuaded himself from stealing from the till, not out of principle but because of the practical inadvisability of any such venture. The narrow confines of the spiritual lives of these Dubliners are mirrored in the material universe: for someone who lives "at a little distance from his body" (Pa 108) and considers himself to have been "outcast from life's feast" (Pa 117) to contemplate the criminal act implies not only a disregard for the class ethic, but a purposefully thought-out disdain for the validity of that ethic.

What ostensibly appears to be the firm rock of economic stability proves particularly vulnerable: Joyce's counterpartite pattern sharply contrasts the victor and the vanquished, the loser quickly losing all while the winner is slowly deprived of his spoils. If Jimmy Doyle's father is the epitome of success as a butcher, having attained wealth and status ("He had also been fortunate enough to secure some of the police contracts and in the end he had become rich enough to be alluded to in the Dublin newspapers as a merchant prince" – Af 43), then his diminished counterpart is Polly Mooney's father, the defunct butcher who was now "obliged to enlist himself as a sheriff's man" (Bo 61) – even their odd relationships with the Law are counterpoised. Allowing for individual strength of character, Mr Doyle exhibits no significant lapses, while Mr Mooney's weakness was drink: "He drank, plundered the till, ran headlong into debt. It was no use making him take the pledge: he was sure to break out again a few days after. By fighting his wife in the presence of customers and by buying bad meat he ruined his business" (Bo 61). The emphasis here is exclusively on the effect on his function as a businessman, not on his health, personality, family relationships, ethical values or spiritual state.

As much as Mr Mooney was irrevocably compromised by his drinking, Mr Doyle had made an important compromise in order to succeed: he "had begun life as an advanced Nationalist, had modified his views early" (Af 43), which easily accounts for the police contracts. Mooney, on the other hand, could not modify his habitual drinking, and consequently ruined not just himself but his business. Not that Doyle remains totally invulnerable: what mistakes he may have avoided making, his son makes in his place. During the hectic events of "After the Race" Jimmy drunkenly gambles away what must be assumed to be a large portion of his patrimony, partly because in the presence of the Englishman Routh, Jimmy "felt the buried zeal of his father wake to life within him: he aroused the torpid Routh at last" (Af 46). Also in contrast to the intemperate Mr Mooney, "A Mother" introduces Mr Kearney, the successful bootmaker on Ormond Quay who can afford to send his family away on holiday to the fashionable resorts, but for all his solid masculine presence and status he can do little to prevent Mr Fitzpatrick and the Committee from denying his daughter her contracted fee.

The precariousness of even the most staunchly comfortable of the middle class is intimated throughout *Dubliners*, but nowhere as richly and poignantly as in "The Dead", where the Morkans display the full panoply of their solid position. Available for scrutiny is an impressive array of food, the goose and the ham and the spiced beef, the jellies and the jams, the nuts and fruit and chocolates and sweets, the port and the sherry, and particularly the controlled and orderly arrangement of the drinks on the piano: "three squads of bottles of stout and ale and minerals, drawn up according to the colours of their uniforms, the first two black, with brown and red labels, the third and smallest squad white, with transverse green sashes" (De 197). The Morkans have main-tained the full measure of their genteel circumstances, their Christmastime party the exhibition of their sustained success ("For years and years it had gone off in splendid style as long as anyone could remember" – De 175–6), but now Mary Jane is giving music lessons, and her aunts are very careful to ensure that her pupils "got the best slices" (De 197), since they came from wealthy, prominent families "on the Kingstown and Dalkey line" (De 176). The death of Pat Morkan – there is no surviving male Morkan – meant that they had had to sell their house in Stoney Batter, and although they still "believed in eating well; the best of everything: diamond-bone sirloins, three-shilling tea and the best bottled stout" (De 176), they are now reduced to living in a "dark gaunt house on Usher's Island, the upper part of which they rented from Mr Fulham, the corn-factor on the ground floor" (De 176). The landlord, incidentally, is not present at the Morkans' soirée, and the implication may be that his social level is below theirs or that his economic level is above theirs. Mr Fulham is one of several "missing" people who go unmentioned in "The Dead", a ghost by absence.

"THE CALCULATION OF COPPERS"

In the Dublin world perhaps only death takes precedence over household economics, as witness the events of "The Sisters", where the protagonist is allowed a relatively finance-free existence, too young to understand circumstances around him in economic terms. Not that he is unaware of relative degrees of wealth and poverty: the household in which he lives can afford to offer casual visitors like Old Cotter "a pick of that leg of mutton" (Si 11), an instance of Irish hospitality in which there is actually a leg of mutton readily available, while his perceptions of the Flynns' business are quite exact: "It was an unassuming shop,registered under the vague name of *Drapery*" (Si 11). He is the one who is the bearer of the regular gift of snuff from his aunt to Father Flynn, perhaps in payment for whatever tutorial the priest was providing. In his own terms the boy is conscious of the donation as a present, and from Eliza Flynn he hears the expression of gratitude offered to his aunt, "you, ma'am, sending him his snuff" (Si 16). Whatever the level of sophistication with which he comprehends these matters, there is no overlooking his ability to perceive "how clumsily her skirt was hooked at the back and how the heels of her cloth boots were trodden down all to one side" (Si 14) – this on a local entrepeneur who sells such items as children's bootees and repairs umbrellas. (A classic symptom of the devalued life of the peddler is an inability to provide for oneself and one's family that service which one provides for others.)

For the child even the most basic exchange of coppers does not visibly take place. Instead, he apprehends a world of barter, donation, charity, and – when all else fails – doing without (as symbolized by the frequent noticings of the empty grate in the Flynn dwelling). Bits of mutton are exchanged for worldly wisdom and advice; High Toast snuff periodically donated or exchanged for lessons; biscuits and sherry offered to guests at a wake; flowers are brought by Father O'Rourke and candlesticks loaned from the chapel. No one can avoid being aware that certain expenses must have been incurred (the woman who comes in to wash the body is paid for her services; the sherry and cream crackers had to be bought; the newspaper announcement paid for), but the polite world of the *petit bourgeois* does not allow for direct references to such money matters, while the boy apparently remains oblivious of them, although now obliquely aware of simony – which he visualizes as a person rather than a concept or the tangibles of a concept. He knows that Cotter has had experiences in a distillery, but to him this implies "faints and worms" (Si 10), rather than an occupation. It is a world in which Father Flynn's life is bartered for an "eternal reward" (Si 16), but in which the boy is not privy to the exchange of coins of the realm, unlike his successors in "An Encounter" and "Araby". There is still an aura of innocence about so young a child, even as a dweller in the city, and it manifests itself quite specifically in terms of household economics.

There is no evidence that the boy knows the price of a packet of High Toast, but he will soon learn that money is needed for a day's miching – and the price of a ticket to the Araby Bazaar. Whereas the opening childhood story is conspicuously innocent of any form of currency, the next two graduate from a song of sixpence to a concert of two shillings. Yet, while "An Encounter" suggests a surfeit of "a bob and a tanner instead of a bob" (En 22), "Araby" records the frustrations evolving from the insufficiency of a mere florin. That the protagonist and his two school-mates are easily able to amass sixpence each to use for a day away from school attests to the relative comforts of their family incomes, which translates into social status by the repeated reminders that they are not National School pupils but day students at a Jesuit institution – apparently Belvedere College. From the first the narrator assumes an exalted position in regard to the sixpences, collecting and holding Mahony's and Leo Dillon's money, while showing his own to them. His role as banker qualifies him for James Duffy's profession in later life, and just as Duffy is reluctant to appropriate imprudently from his own bank, the boy is uncertain as to the proper disposition of Leo Dillon's money once Dillon fails to show up. Mahony, however, is quite clearheaded and definite ("That's forfeit. . . . And so much the better for us" – En 22), demonstrating a basic characteristic of capitalist enterprise – which the narrator hardly objects to once Mahony makes his point. For their refreshment they buy biscuits, chocolate and raspberry lemonade, but never indicate how much they have spent or whether they have encroached on the forfeited share.

Mahony and his mate now treat all the money as their own, casual about how they came by it and relaxed in how they spend it: money seems not to be a problem and they expend little thought on the subject. For the youth in "Araby" the realities are more pressing. Not only must he depend on his uncle's largesse but also wait for his uncle's arrival home before receiving it (and there is little doubt that the uncle has been delayed in the pubs spending his own pay in his own way). Nor does the florin prove sufficient. What may have been a generous donation for the uncle translates as a paltry sum for the recipient, for whom the time of childhood is running out and the ensuing needs are not met by his role as a dependant. The transition is clearly marked: "I could not find any sixpenny entrance and, fearing that the bazaar would be closed, I passed in quickly through a turnstile, handing a shilling to a weary-looking man" (Ar 34). The *rites de passage* from the sixpence childhood to the twice-sixpence demanded by the boy's new status as a male intent on buying a gift for Mangan's sister are made difficult by the discrepancy between his own estimation of his new position and the time it takes for his credentials to be validated. The adult world has failed to notice the immediate change in him; time's delay impedes his progress toward accelerated maturity; and his finances are inadequate to bankroll his anticipated lifestyle. None the less, he has become wise in the ways of the economic world, choosing a third-class train carriage for economy but a shilling entrance for expediency, and comprehending the chasm between what an impressive present would cost and the money now remaining in his pocket.

"PUT BUT MONEY IN THY PURSE"

An important transition is effected when the stories of adolescence succeed those of childhood. Although Eveline is only nineteen years old, her role as wage-earner is an essential characteristic, and her salary the only specifically quantified one in all of *Dubliners*. The point has been reached where children no longer receive money, but must earn it. While remaining children within the familial context, they are also expected to donate to household expenses – a condition that Stephen Dedalus in *A Portrait* accepted with enthusiasm when awarded his prize money but which Stephen in *Ulysses* scrupulously avoids. It is apparent that Mr Hill anticipates the Simon Dedalus of *Ulysses*, and the uncle in "Araby" was a mild and reasonable head of household by comparison with either of them. Eveline's recollection of the Saturday evening ritual indicates what a battle royal pay night in Dublin can be:

the invariable squabble for money on Saturday nights had begun to weary her unspeakably. She always gave her entire wages – seven shillings – and Harry always sent up what he could but the trouble was to get any money from her father. He said she used to squander the money, that she had no head, that he wasn't going to give her his hard-earned money to throw about the streets, and much more, for he was usually fairly bad of a Saturday night. In the end he would give her the money and ask her had she any intention of buying Sunday's dinner. Then she had to rush out as quickly as she could and do her marketing. (Ev 38)

In a capsule of scrupulous meanness collapsing a long scene of sustained action and dialogue, this potent passage not only reveals Eveline's exact contribution (a seemingly unnecessary repetition of her weekly wage), but conceals the amounts offered by brother Harry (variable) and Mr Hill (perhaps also variable).

The mystery surrounding the exact nature of their donations adumbrates the conditions of the following story, "After the Race", where a contrasting atmosphere of relatively high finances smoke-screens the particulars of pounds, shillings and pence, although it might be assumed that the financial currencies involved are detailed more appropriately in guineas. How much money did Mr Doyle make in order to qualify as a merchant prince of butchers? How much did he pass over to his son Jimmy to invest in the automotive enterprise? And how much did Jimmy actually lose in the card game? Adjacent to a world in which every sixpence counts, and every seven-shilling salary is carefully parcelled out for necessities, what price Jimmy's squandered patrimony? The mores of the middle class dictate that monetary discussions may be a commonplace, but that one's salary figures are shrouded in secrecy. The bland reiteration of Eveline Hill's seven shillings is hardly accidental in a work in which exceedingly few items are ever divulged more than once – and many important pieces of factual information totally withheld. Eveline's wages are an open secret (her father certainly knows the exact amount) since she is not the sole determiner of her own financial situation. At nineteen she is still a dependent member of her family's household despite her wage-earning capacity, a *child* not unlike the boy in "An Encounter" and "Araby", rather than an *adult* like Jimmy Doyle.

After "Eveline" salary figures are unavailable: we never learn how much Mr Leonard pays Bob Doran, or what Chandler earns at the King's Inns or Farrington at Crosbie and Alleyne's, or James Duffy at the private bank on Baggot Street. We can assume that

Maria's position at the *Dublin by Lamplight* laundry is essentially a charitable arrangement that includes bed and board, and although she meticulously doles out her expenditures for the evening out ("in the purse were two half-crowns and some coppers. She would have five shillings clear after paying tram fare" – Cl 100), she does pride herself on being financially independent to a significant degree: "She arranged in her mind all she was going to do and thought how much better it was to be independent and to have your own money in your pocket" (Cl 102). Such solvency, however, may be self-deceptive. Like others who feel secure in their jobs or smug in their accumulated assets (Doran, Doyle), she faces an uncertain future: she muses that often Joe Donnelly had "wanted her to go and live with them; but she would have felt herself in the way . . . and she had become accustomed to the life of the laundry" (Cl 100). That Mrs Donnelly (the actual source of Maria's apprehensions about being "in the way") should predict that "Maria would enter a convent before the year was out" (Cl 105) does not bode well for Maria's capacity to continue working in the laundry kitchen. We can only speculate on how close she is to dotage, but there is a comic echo in her night's "miching" of the boys in "An Encounter", as she parcels out her money for penny cakes and a plumcake. Maria's generosity drastically depletes her financial resources. "Two-and-four" for the plumcake almost annihilates one of her half-crowns, and "a dozen of mixed penny cakes" (Cl 102) almost halves the other. And the acrimony caused by the inquest over the lost cakes destroys whatever goodwill the purchase should have bought.

Maria's meagre five shillings may have been sufficient for an evening out – she still comes away with one shilling and eight pence in her purse – but Farrington in "Counterparts" senses that it would not be enough for his "spell of riot" (Co 91). Having spent his last penny for the afternoon glass of porter, Farrington considers the problem of financing his night's "miching", and decides to pawn his watch. Offered only a crown (five shillings), he holds out for and manages to get six shillings from Terry Kelly's clerk, yet that too eventually proves minimal considering the present state of "the barometer of his emotional nature" (Co 91). One can only guess how much money would ultimately have been necessary for Farrington to have arrived at the desired degree of drunkenness, or whether his emotional nature might not have precluded any possible success in obliterating his awareness of disaster. None the less, a careful tracking of the trickle of shillings and pence over the course of the evening in Davy Byrne's, the Scotch House and John Mulligan's indicates how futile his Sisyphean venture was destined to be.

Lacking Lenehan's talent for "holding himself nimbly at the borders of the company until he was included in a round" (Tw 50), Farrington establishes himself at the centre of the company with his repeatable retort to Mr Alleyne as his trump card. Yet, between the aggressive thrusts of Higgins in Davy Byrne's and Weathers in Mulligan's, Farrington is diminished in both battles of wits and strength, and watches his proceeds go primarily for the drinks of others. Allowing for the obvious gaps in narrative detailing, we can clock him as having consumed nine drinks, probably all hot whisky punches, and having paid for at least fifteen, plus the extra expense of Weathers' extravagant tastes for diluting his whisky with Apollinaris water. He has spent five shillings and ten pence ("he had only twopence in his pocket" – Co 97), having failed not only to capitalize on his piece of arrogant wit by being the recipient of free drinks, but also to break even. His remaining twopence would barely provide a raspberry lemonade for a schoolboy out on an afternoon's adventure.

Just how precarious the Farrington family finances must be can only be surmised from several categories of evidence: that he is virtually penniless on this particular day; that his credit is not good at his own place of employment; that he is in danger of losing that employment; that he has a large family to support. The logical contrast is with someone like James Duffy (good job, no dependants, no expensive habits), while Thomas Chandler suggests himself as an even more logical counterpart. In character he more closely resembles Duffy than Farrington, except that he has married – and the implications are that pretty-faced Annie requires a good bit more to keep her content. Whereas personal finances were paramount throughout "Counterparts", they make a late appearance in "A Little Cloud", but once on the scene they quickly become diagnostic. The almost too-casual statement that "To save money they kept no servant but Annie's younger sister Monica came for an hour or so in the morning and an hour or so in the evening to help" (Li 82) drops into place to suggest that Annie *expects* domestic service regardless of Chandler's salary level. That she also expects parcels of coffee from Bewley's follows immediately after, and she receives husbandly gifts of summer blouses that cost "ten and elevenpence" (Li 83) – obviously an item of clothing out of the question for Eveline Hill. Although she made quite a show of objecting to the outrageous price, she none the less chose to keep the blouse because she was so delighted with it. Annie's penchant for pretty things mirrors her husband having been tempted irrevocably by her pretty face, and we have only to read the furniture to ascertain just how fixed Chandler's eroding position apparently is:

> He looked coldly into the eyes of the photograph and they answered coldly. Certainly they were pretty and the face itself was pretty. But he found something mean in it. . . .
>
> He caught himself up at the question and glanced nervously round the room. He found something mean in the pretty furniture which he had bought for his house on the hire system. Annie had chosen it herself and it reminded him of her. It too was prim and pretty. A dull resentment against his life awoke within him. Could he not escape from his little house?   (Li 83)

Chandler's entrapment among the furniture is already determined, while Bob Doran faces the inevitability of the sprung trap of pretty-faced Polly Mooney. The indications are that Doran's job may well be a better one than Chandler's (after all, he can afford fifteen shillings a week at Mrs Mooney's boarding house), but a glance ahead into *Ulysses* corroborates the sealed fate suggested at the end of "The Boarding House".

"I PAID MY WAY"

Financial security, by comparison, sits particularly well on Gabriel Conroy. As is the case with all the principal wage-earners in *Dubliners*, no salary figures are ever quoted, but the aura of well-being that surrounds Gabriel (as reflected by "his broad, well-filled shirt-front" – De 218) attests to solid economic stability. The house in Monkstown, the servant Bessie, the expense of a night at the Gresham, and numerous other indicators add up to the most affluent kind of burgher this side of that merchant prince of butchers. It is clear that he can afford to be generous with small amounts of money, having loaned Freddie Malins a pound when he went into the Christmas card business, and now presenting Lily with "a coin" as a holiday gratuity. But most characteristic of the relaxed state of his family finances is his attitude toward book reviewing:

> It was true that he wrote a literary column every Wednesday in *The Daily Express,* for which he was paid fifteen shillings. . . . The books he received for review were almost more welcome than the paltry cheque. He loved to feel the covers and run over the pages of newly printed books. Nearly every day when his teaching in the college was ended he used to wander down the quays to the second-hand booksellers, to Hickey's on Bachelor's Walk, to Webb's or Massey's on Aston's Quay, or to O'Clohissey's in the by-street.   (De 188)

Perhaps it is only annoyance with Molly Ivors that causes him to regard fifteen shillings as paltry, but we can easily estimate what the amount as a weekly increment would mean to Eveline or Farrington or Chandler or Tom Kernan.

Kernan's income depends to a certain degree on his sales commissions, a state of uncertainty not uncommon among a segment of the middle class. Unlike the elder Doyle or Mr Kearney, apparently a successful entrepreneur as a "bootmaker on Ormond Quay" (Mo 137), Kernan retains his status as a member of the *salariat* dependent on customers to a greater extent since he does not actually own the commodity that he sells. As a petit bourgeois he has his delusions of grandeur, and although "he would walk to the end of Thomas Street and back again to book even a smaller order" (Gr 156), he assumes that on the basis of his fastidious clothes (second-hand, we learn from evidence in *Ulysses*) he was eligible for even higher class status:

> Mr Kernan was a commercial traveller of the old school which believed in the dignity of its calling. He had never been seen in the city without a silk hat of some decency and a pair of gaiters. By grace of these two articles of clothing, he said, a man could always pass muster. He carried on the tradition of his Napoleon, the great Blackwhite, whose memory he evoked at times by legend and mimicry. Modern business methods had spared him only so far as to allow him a little office in Crowe Street on the window blind of which was written the name of his firm with the address – London, E.C.   (Gr 153–4)

Kernan is appropriately dressed for a fall from a great height (down the lavatory steps, down the economic ladder), and on the occasion of his perilous and precipitous descent he is temporarily separated from his silk hat. Like his hat ("dinged" and "battered" – Gr 151, 152), Kernan is deemed reparable: all the King's horses and men (Power and Cunningham are "employed in the Royal Irish Constabulary Office in Dublin Castle" – Gr 154) are witnessed at work on his restoration. As a serious drinker Mr Kernan runs the risk that ruined Mr Mooney; as a tea-taster he has damaged the one physical property on which his livelihood depends, his tongue. Employed by a London firm he may long since have lessened his position in converting to Catholicism in order to marry someone of that faith: the implications are also that he has married socially beneath him, and the large number of children engendered must also have been a continual drain on his financial resources. In *Ulysses* he reappears upright and functioning in his profession, apparently unchanged directly by his visit to the Jesuit church retreat, and more likely sustained somewhat by his allegiance to the Freemasons instead, since at the funeral he is still giving lip-service to the religion of his origins rather than of his conversion. His restored tongue wags quite a bit, making him the butt of bar-room pleasantries, and spirits are still hot in his mouth – he has just had a drink when we first see him again. None the less, Tom Kernan is still hanging on financially, silk-hatted and gaitered, and retaining his claims to bourgeois respectability.

"Grace" is the one story of public life that offers a larger cross-section of the gainfully employed bourgeoisie. Kernan as a salesman is augmented by Fogarty as a single entrepreneur, "a modest grocer", but not without his own background of economic difficulties:

> He had failed in business in a licensed house in the city because his financial condition had constrained him to tie himself to second-class distillers and brewers. He had opened a small shop on Glasnevin Road where, he flattered himself, his manners would ingratiate him with the housewives of the district.
>
> (Gr 166)

Fogarty, of course, is the uninvited and unexpected guest, a comforter from outside the small cabal enjoined by the two public servants from Dublin Castle that includes C. P. M'Coy, also a Dublin city official of sorts.

M'Coy is the *chosen* outsider, a man who has held more jobs than there are wage-earners in the room. His professional career in itself provides a catalogue of middle-class Dublin employment that encapsulates the era:

> M'Coy had been at one time a tenor of some reputation. . . . His line of life had not been the shortest distance between two points and for short periods he had been driven to live by his wits. He had been a clerk in the Midland Railway, a canvasser for advertisements for *The Irish Times* and for *The Freeman's Journal*, a town traveller for a coal firm on commission, a private inquiry agent, a clerk in the office of the Sub-Sheriff and he had recently become secretary to the City Coroner.   (Gr 158)

Composite M'Coy is almost the quintessential bourgeois Dubliner, with more jobs in his past than even his presumed successor at the *Freeman*, Leopold Bloom, and more real jobs that those ticked off by Stephen Dedalus in *A Portrait* for his insubstantial father. If the events of 16 June 1904 follow close upon those of "Grace", it is gratifying to note that he is *still* working for the Coroner, for with obviously less wit than Lenehan he would not make much of a go of living by them. Almost all of the participants in the events of this story reappear in *Ulysses* in their same occupational capacities (Kernan, Power, Cunningham, M'Coy), except for unfortunate Fogarty, mentioned only once when Power asks ominously, "I wonder how is our friend Fogarty getting on" (Ha 454) – again presumably out of business.

THE HAVES AND THE HAVE-NOTS

In contradistinction to the more secure "employees" observed in "Grace" are the cluster of threadbare members of the lower middle class holed up in the "Ivy Day" committee room, where they have temporary but hardly satisfactory employment canvassing for Tierney. Whatever their regular vocations may be – and there is no indication anywhere in the story for any of the four canvassers –

they are obviously not practising them at the moment, but have been taken on by the political candidate as hired help, disgruntled at their menial status. Two of them, John Henchy and Mat O'Connor, play out their existences in *Dubliners* and do not make the transition into *Ulysses*; of the others, Crofton is revealed as a "pensioner out of the collector general's" (Cy 1589–90), but his elevated position was never in doubt since he is a Conservative on loan to Tierney's Nationalists. Bantam Lyons, however, the first character in *Dubliners* to have a prior position in the text, a resident at Mrs Mooney's boarding house, is well displayed in the succeeding text, but primarily as a racing punter and pub customer. (If either of these "vocations" takes precedence for him over the other, on 16 June 1904 it is horse racing, and he may have been abstaining temporarily in order to have the money to lose on Sceptre.) A fifth wheel in the committee room is the intruder, Joe Hynes, another uninvited guest who none the less makes himself very much at home, but seems to have no visible means of support ("he's hard up like the rest of us", says O'Connor – Iv 124), yet in *Ulysses* he is working as a reporter for the *Telegraph*, but borrowing money when short – for the usual purposes.

The supposition seems safe that at least four of the quintet in the room are "between jobs", and considering the concern voiced by O'Connor and Henchy, they desperately need the recompense expected from the candidate. O'Connor's "boots let in the wet" (Iv 119), so that he is not out earning his pay, although he is quick to utter his prayer, "I hope to God he'll not leave us in the lurch tonight" and "I wish he'd turn up with the spondulics" (Iv 121, 122). When Henchy reports "No money, boys" (Iv 122), the matter is not taken lightly since he claims to "expect to find the bailiffs in the hall when I go home" (Iv 124). Hynes, not in Tierney's employ and therefore not expecting anything except a possible bottle of stout, takes the matter of money in his stride, but once he has left he is vilified by Henchy: "Damn it, I can understand a fellow being hard up but what I can't understand is a fellow sponging. Couldn't he have some spark of manhood about him?" (Iv 124). If Tierney intends to keep his promise ("*when I see the work going on properly I won't forget you*" – Iv 123), it may well be a long while before the likes of Mat O'Connor sees the candidate's spondulics, although one can assume that as a representative of the commercial interests in Dublin, Tierney can afford to pay his workers. "What's the difference between a good honest bricklayer and a publican – eh?"

asks Joe Hynes rhetorically, distinguishing between Colgan, who "goes in to represent the labour classes", and Tierney, who "only wants to get some job or other" (Iv 121). The answer to the question that needs no answer is a dozen bottles of stout from Tierney's pub, pseudo-payment that quiets and mollifies, ending any talk of spondulics and bailiffs-in-the-hall.

The reference to Colgan, and Hynes's pronouncement that "The working-man . . . gets all kicks and no halfpence" (Iv 121), are only occasional reminders in *Dubliners* of the existence of the lower classes, except in that odd moment when a down-at-the-heels bourgeois like Lenehan lowers himself to eat in the "Refreshment Bar" in Great Britain Street. Nor is the depressed atmosphere in the committee room, where even the finances of a Catholic priest are suspect ("And how does he knock it out? asked Mr O'Connor" – Iv 126), actually representative of the solid middle class, the domain of the Tierneys and the Croftons. At their best the comfortable burghers can be seen in the Gardiner Street church listening to Father Purdon's sermon, a distinguished congregation of burgesses:

> In a whisper Mr Cunningham drew Mr Kernan's attention to Mr Harford, the moneylender, who sat some distance off, and to Mr Fanning, the registration agent and mayor maker of the city, who was sitting immediately under the pulpit beside one of the newly elected councillors of the ward. To the right sat old Michael Grimes, the owner of three pawnbroker's shops, and Dan Hogan's nephew, who was up for the job in the Town Clerk's office. Farther in front sat Mr Hendrick, the chief reporter of *The Freeman's Journal*, and poor O'Carroll, an old friend of Mr Kernan's, who had been at one time a considerable commercial figure.   (Gr 172–3)

The sociodynamics of the bourgeois maelstrom are apparent in this capsule: those on the way up rubbing shoulders with those on the way down; the dignity of the old commerce (silk hats and gaiters) giving way to the disreputable practices of moneylenders and pawnbrokers; those who purvey their wares to the solvent and those who batten on the poor. (And the publican-politico Tierney may be the unnamed new councillor sandwiched in among them.)

Whereas a dearth of needed spondulics is at the centre of "Ivy Day in the Committee Room", several of the narratives focus quite specifically on the exchange of coins, but no single coin of the realm glistens quite so pervasively in *Dubliners* as Corley's triumphantly revealed half-sovereign, demonstrative, reverberating, representative, symbolic. Whatever our expectations regarding Corley's stratagem and Lenehan's attendant anxieties, the exposure of the gold coin in his palm illuminated under lamplight provides the major obscenity of the book, the most potent instance of simony in secular practice. Other coins pale in association, although they have their own simoniac significances (a forfeited sixpence, an inadequate florin, the small coin tendered as a Christmas gift but serving as a bribe to cover an embarrassing gaucherie, a pawn-broker's clerk's demeaning offer of a crown for a watch). In the manner of miraculous revelation Corley takes up his grandiose pose: "with a grave gesture he extended a hand towards the light and, smiling, opened it slowly to the gaze of his disciple. A small gold coin shone in the palm" (Tw 60). That the coin is intended for a night's carousing to exceed even Farrington's six-shilling expectation goes unstated and needs no statement, and parallels the situation in the Royal Exchange Ward committee room, where no money ever appears but a dozen of stout is introduced as barter for services rendered and dispels all discussion of a missing payment.

Corley-with-coin-in-hand has his ironic return to the stage of the dark Dublin streets when he resurfaces in *Ulysses*, panhandling from Stephen Dedalus. With "Not as much as a farthing to purchase a night's lodgings", and aware of "a decent enough do in the Brazen Head over in Winetavern street . . . for a bob" (Eu 145, 168–70), Corley manages to extract a half-crown from Stephen, who intended to give him "anything up to a bob" (Eu 183), but assuming that the coins in his pocket were pennies, offered two of them. In this comedy of monetary errors Corley is in no position to refuse a coin, pocketing the one large half-crown that serves as a pale reflection of the small gold coin he had once brandished with a flourish gauged to dazzle a disciple. That "Lord John Corley" is desperate enough to ask a highly sceptical Stephen about the possibilities of a job attests to the transitoriness of even a gold coin, much less a half-crown. He begs off, however, when told of an opening to be created by Stephen leaving Mr Deasy's school: "sure I couldn't teach in a school, man. I was never one of your bright ones" (Eu 160–1). In a highly limited job market ("I'd carry a sandwichboard only the girl in the office told me they're full up for the next three weeks, man" – Eu 200–1), where preference may not even depend on skills and attributes, Corley's admitted limitations strongly reduce his possibilities.

"THOUGH SHE'S A FACTORY LASS . . . "

How much more difficult then are the prospects facing women seeking employment in the commercial city of Dublin. Eveline Hill is starting as a shop assistant in the Stores, a menial under Miss Gavan; Maria, decidedly older and probably better connected socially, seems to have the run of the kitchen at the charitable laundry, with the dummy as her menial. And Eveline has no illusions that "her place would be filled up by advertisement" soon enough if she left her job (Ev 37). Proprietors of houses on Baggot Street have their live-in domestic servants, and corn-factors' offices employ typists like Polly Mooney. On the other hand, musical talents in musical Dublin apparently open possibilities not available to the ordinary Evelines and Pollys, yet "A Mother" exemplifies the traps and pitfalls present within that male-dominated profession. Mary Jane as a piano teacher escapes such obstacles by being self-employed, but must defer socially to her well-heeled pupils; her aunt Julia, however, has encountered an unexpected aspect of male domination when the Catholic Church elected "to turn out the women out of the choirs that have slaved there all their lives and put little whipper-snappers of boys over their heads" (De 194). Even such donated service can run the risk of undeserved termination, and this unusual incident marring the yuletide festivities adds to the accumulated bits of evidence that indicate that the Morkans are very much in economic decline, existing now with an excess of emphasis on the past and but diminishing prospects for the future.

The economic forces operative in turn-of-the-century Dublin, as elsewhere in capitalist society, function along masculine lines of development and entrenchment, and that floor of the "dark gaunt house" (De 176) occupied exclusively by the three Morkan women seems definitely in its twilight years. If we read the conclusion of "The Dead" prophetically, the Morkans may be entertaining in grand style for the last time. Kate and Julia are both fatherless and brotherless: no male surviving relative exists as a wage-earner for them, and with their niece they live in isolation from those factors that generate wealth. (Like Maria they apparently face declining financial prospects, but also like her they are most likely under sentence of imminent death, which would make their financial considerations moot.) Julia's rendition of "Arrayed for the Bridal" may indeed have been superb, in which case it may, despite all assumptions to the contrary, also have the grandeur of a swansong, and she herself admits that "Thirty years ago I hadn't a bad voice as voices go" (De 194). Mary Jane, apparently also quite accomplished, seems to have no real chance of capturing an audience, as her performances at the soirée seems to indicate: "Gabriel could not listen while Mary Jane was playing her Academy piece, full of runs and difficult passages. . . . He liked music but the piece she was playing had no melody for him and he doubted whether it had any melody for the other listeners" (De 186). Assuming that Gabriel is more discerning than the others, his censure can be taken to be diagnostic, but not necessarily that Mary Jane's abilities are deficient – there is the good possibility that her level of attainment has surpassed that of her less intellectual guests.

The Morkan musical talents are merely peripheral counters in the financial scheme of things in a Dublin that is essentially commercial and only minimally industrialized, its commerce an extension of its agricultural hinterlands. Julia and Kate Morkan had never been educated to replace the men who made and sustained the family's fortunes, and as much as we may laugh with Gabriel at grandfather Morkan's glue (or starch) mill, it was the mill that paid for the house in Stoney Batter and ensured a succession of diamond-bone steaks for the Morkan table. The training which made the horse, the "never-to-be-forgotten Johnny" (De 207), hypnotically drive the mill has not been lavished on the Morkan women, and music lessons, although an indicator of their genteel pretensions, do not provide as much income as glue or starch. A concert career, however, can assure decidedly better prospects, yet Miss Devlin apparently did not have sufficient talent for such a possibility – or no such possibility was presented to her. The important years of her young adulthood are glossed over in a succinctly economical pair of sentences of scrupulous meanness: "She had been educated in a high-class convent where she had learned French and music. . . . When she came to the age of marriage she was sent out to many houses where her playing and ivory manners were much admired" (Mo 136). The "age of marriage" apparently precludes all other options for a young woman of Miss Devlin's class, and it is as subsequent that she should marry an older, established, solid citizen like Mr Kearney, who was "sober, thrifty and pious" (Mo 137), as it is that she should later devote herself to putting her daughter Kathleen on the stage.

Boots, like glue and starch, can be parlayed into profits that afford holidays for one's wife and daughter in Skerries or Howth or Greystone, yet the bootmaker's genteel environment and his wife's ivory manners fail to prepare either of them for the world of Fitzpatrick and Holohan and the Committee, and the rules by which they function. (Mr Kearney more probably belongs to the school of Kernan and "poor O'Carroll", while the Dublin musical world is dominated by a harder, more cut-throat clan – the infighting here is particularly vicious because the stakes are so low.) Ivory manners prove brittle against the immovable force of the Committee intent on cutting its losses, and Mr Kearney's masculine presence effete, despite the traditional bourgeois values of sobriety, thriftiness and piety. Bourgeois ideals have been so corrupted and compromised in the world of the *Eire Abu* Society that they correspond to those of the politics of the Royal Exchange Ward, where, as Henchy asserts, "You must owe the City Fathers money nowadays if you want to be made Lord Mayor. Then they'll make you Lord Mayor" (Iv 127), or the politics of the nation, where, as O'Connor insists, a certain "patriot" is a "fellow now that'd sell his country for fourpence – ay – and go down on his bended knees and thank the Almighty Christ he had a country to sell" (Iv 125). Fourpence may not be the highest monetary value discernible in the financial world of *Dubliners*, but it serves adequately as the metaphoric equivalent of the scratching among the citizenry for the necessary pounds, shillings and pence.

5

Double Binds: Talismans of Immaturity

It doubles itself in the middle of his life, reflects itself in another, repeats itself, protasis, epitasis, catastasis, catastrophe. It repeats itself again.

(SC 1002–4)

Ever would he wander, selfcompelled, to the extreme limit of his cometary orbit, beyond the fixed stars and variable suns and telescopic planets, astronomical waifs and strays, to the extreme boundary of space, passing from land to land, among peoples, amid events. Somewhere imperceptibly, he would hear and somehow reluctantly, suncompelled, obey the summons of recall.

(It 2013–18)

THE BOY IN THE GAP

The "separateness" that exists between the stories of the "unified" scheme of *Dubliners* only becomes apparent on the rare occasion when a character who appears in an earlier story is mentioned in a later one, so that we become aware of how contained each of the narratives had been. Yet many aspects of Dublin life and its interpersonal relationships invisibly bind and interconnect the participants in that paralytic world of the Catholic bourgeoisie that is Joyce's Dublin. In parallel proportions each of the protagonists is bound within his or her own world, caught in binds both of their own making and externally conditioned under circumstances at once indeterminate and overdetermined. The spaces that separate individuals often narrow dangerously and yet persist as unbridgeable, and the Dublin that becomes apparent is simultaneously a diffuse metropolis and a provincial town.

The space that forms between "The Sisters" and "An Encounter" not only separates the two stories in time and locale but establishes invisible linkages, like a vista of clear air transmitting sound waves of connectedness. The topographic interval between the home areas of the two boys who appear as the protagonists remains vague, with only minimal indicators (Father Flynn residing in Great Britain Street, the Dillons attending Mass in Gardiner Street) bringing them close, but not binding them inexorably. At various instances in "An Encounter" it becomes apparent that details regarding the boy's home life are not forthcoming, that gaps persist in the narrative, leaving him as likely to be living with an aunt and uncle, rather than parents, as is the boy of "The Sisters". Nor is there a name attached to this particular boy either: the deployment of the first-person singular for narrational presentation avoids the assignment of a name for the central character of the three stories of childhood, and even direct nominative address to him by others gets elliptically bypassed. Negative evidence along these lines leaves open, without actually asserting, the continuous presence of the same boy in both "The Sisters" and "An Encounter", allowing us to choose freely between separate and discrete narrative packaging and individual developments of specific protagonists – or a preference for the simultaneous retention of both possibilities.

The "problem" of nomenclature calls attention to itself even when names are not mysteriously withheld or tantalizingly dangled as incorrect. The boy in "An Encounter" takes it upon himself to assign a pair of pseudonyms, for his companion as well as for himself: "In case he asks us for our names", he instructs Mahony, "let you be Murphy and I'll be Smith" (En 26). Whatever the boy's surname actually is, it is certainly not Smith, since no one would conceivably assume his real name as a disguise; nor is his name Murphy, since he would also not use his own name as a disguise for his companion. The easy association of Mahony and Murphy, that most common of all Irish names, suggests a possible pattern in the namer's thinking process: that his own name bears a similar association with the Smith pseudonym (Murphy is to Mahony as X is to Smith). A more subtle motivation, however, may be operative in the naming process: that the boy is thoroughly "disguising" a name not unlike Mahony through the use of the quite dissimilar "Smith". Just as both Mahony and Murphy proclaim a profound Irishness, so Smith veers toward a distinctly more *Anglo*-Irish posture. In one stroke the boy may be protecting himself from the "queer old josser" and bettering himself socially in contrast to Mahony. His closing confession ("in my heart I had always despised him a little" – En 28) confirms a snobbishness not inconsistent with the choice of a "superior" name for himself.

The space that either separates or bridges "An Encounter" and "Araby" contains the same potentials as the blank between the first two stories: distancing for discrete characterization or the setting of the stage for further developments. Once again the topographical boundaries, the naming of the *dramatis personae* and the family circumstances are allowed either to establish or disrupt the possibility of continuous identity for the protagonist. The opening directional indication in "Araby" ("North Richmond Street, being blind, was a quiet street" – Ar 29) locates the boy's dwelling for the first time, providing a focal centre from which the distances to Gardiner Street, Great Britain Street and the Canal Bridge are sufficiently reasonable – a setting of boundaries. (Calling attention to the "former tenant" (Ar 29), however, suggests a recent occupancy, a sense of shifting boundaries.) Anonymity continues to "protect" the central character, and once again the only family life that exists for him is with an aunt and uncle. The lone instance of the use of the uncle's name in the first story (Jack) has no corollary in the third story, the negative evidence preserving the purity of extended narrative. The unnamed uncle in "Araby" sends his nephew off to the Araby Bazaar not only with the opening lines of "The Arab's Farewell to his Steed", but also with *"All work and no play makes Jack a dull boy"* (Ar 34) – certainly no indicator that the boy's name is Jack, but comically off-centre if the uncle's name is.

The same name will surface again, by a process of economical employment of a tightly limited series of given names in the *Dubliners* narratives: "Ivy Day in the Committee Room" introduces "Old Jack", the caretaker, whose own continuing narration concerns his profligate son. "I sent him to the Christian Brothers and I done what I could for him", he complains (Iv 119), recalling the opening of "Araby": "North Richmond Street, being blind, was a quiet street except at the hour when the Christian Brothers' School set the boys free" (Ar 29).

The important events of all three initiating stories take place away from the boy's residence, in the first two at the Flynns' and on the road to the Pigeon House (which proves to be "out of bounds"), although the North Richmond Street house in the third plays a far more prominent role (the boy frustratingly "bound" within its confines), its dimensions charted and its "high cold empty gloomy rooms" (Ar 33) evocative. The fire before which Mrs Mercer sits replicates the fire before which Old Cotter sat in "The Sisters", the Cotter/Mercer analogues also binding the narratives together: "She was an old garrulous woman, a pawnbroker's widow, who collected used stamps for some pious purpose" (Ar 33); he was a "Tiresome old fool" with "endless stories about the distillery" (Si 10).

The newly deceased Father Flynn of "The Sisters" projects his ghostly presence upon the house in "Araby", where the boy is aware that "The former tenant of our house, a priest, died in the back drawing-room" (Ar 29). The separate identities of the priest who died in his sisters' house in Great Britain Street and the priest who died in the back drawing-room of his house in North Richmond Street strengthens rather than weakens the single identity of the boy in the companion stories, since the extensions of time can allow the same boy to live in three separate residences at the instances of the events of the three narratives. The books associated with Father Flynn ("he told me that the fathers of the Church had written books as thick as the *Post Office Directory*" – Si 13) have their ironic echo in the "few paper-covered books" that belonged to the dead priest of "Araby": "*The Abbot*, by Walter Scott, *The Devout Communicant* and *The Memoirs of Vidocq*" (Ar 29).

Considering the vague entries on the anonymous priest's reading matter (the three books among the litter of "old useless papers" – Ar 29), uncomfortably open possibilities continually suggest themselves: abandoned books or retained books? rejected or cherished? Of the three bibliographic clues for identification, three categories of information are presented: only one book has both a title and author, a second only a title, the third a title that contains and implies the locus of authorship. A Gothic novel may well concern itself with Roman Catholic ecclesiasts and remain luridly unreligious and anti-Catholic; a volume with the rather common title of *The Devout Communicant* can be either Catholic or Protestant, and if the latter, can be virulently anti-Catholic; the memoirs of an illustrative person may be edifying and uplifting, even if the subject is a police official, but Eugène François Vidocq was a criminal before founding the Sûreté and probably remained one even after. That he had his existence on both sides of the law parallels the hypothetical communicants on either side of the Christian fence and the ironic duality of the religious setting of *The Abbot*. None of the three volumes necessarily escapes censure, and the image of a pitifully naive priest, unlucky perhaps in his judging of books by their covers, contrasts with the highly intellectual Father Flynn, although the naive priest may have died a contented man, rather than a disappointed one whose life was, "you might say, crossed" (Si 17).

What does it take to bring a sensitive young boy to the vortex of "anguish and anger", to lacerate himself with the image of his own self "as a creature driven and derided by vanity" (Ar 35)? The singular experience of the "Araby" context accounts for annoyance with the delays imposed by a parental figure, the insensitivity and self-absorption of the drunken uncle; the hopelessness of infatuation with a remote madonna, the captive of her religion rather than the responding beloved appreciative of her knight errant; the callow flirtatiousness of a shop girl with lecherous Englishmen, an ironic echo of his own disguised sexual awakening. Measuring the severity of the self-accusation with the seriousness of his own transgressions requires a delicate – and highly subjective – valency, one that might sustain itself better when the traumas conditioned in "The Sisters" and "An Encounter" are added to the scales. In the first story, when a stunned silence takes command of the closing scene, the voice of the narrating central intelligence disappears from contention, locked out of the boundaries of the experience. Instead, only the voice of one of the sisters, Eliza, monopolizes the indictment of Father Flynn, the boy's aunt acting as instigating agent (the other sister, Nannie, after serving as hostess, "leaned her head against the sofa-pillow and seemed about to fall asleep" – Si 16). Mirroring Nannie "abstracted out" is the situation of the boy himself: her role of server of sherry and cream crackers is balanced by his acceptance of the first and rejection of the second. Thereafter, "No one spoke; we all gazed at the empty fireplace" (Si 15). The communal silence is a preamble to Nannie's permanent silence and the boy's abdication of his role as commenting narrator of his own experience.

Silences are ominous in "The Sisters". Halfway through the visitation scene, the boy seeks a way to fill the silence although he has given up his narrational commentary (an odd reversal for someone who was so "vocal" in denouncing Old Cotter as a fool and imbecile):

A silence took possession of the little room and, under cover of it, I approached the table and tasted my sherry and then returned quietly to my chair in the corner. Eliza seemed to have fallen into a deep revery. We waited respectfully for her to break the silence.

(Si 17)

Stealth, discomfort, obsequiousness, even an aura of veneration as if approaching an altar, mark the boy's demeanour, repressing his reactions to the enormity of the indictment of the priest by his well-intentioned sister, which the dead man cannot answer. The concluding silence, just prior to the final verdict on Father Flynn's demented behaviour in the confession box, is obliquely filled by the boy's "external" narration:

> She stopped suddenly as if to listen. I too listened; but there was no sound in the house: and I knew that the old priest was lying still in his coffin as we had seen him, solemn and truculent in death, an idle chalice on his breast.   (Si 18)

A component factor of "anguish and anger" may well be accumulating beneath the constraint in the boy's social behaviour, beneath the silence that covers his internalized reactions, resolving itself in the Araby Bazaar, where he "recognized a silence like that which pervades a church after a service" (Ar 34).

"An Encounter" contrasts significantly with "The Sisters" in that the boy retains his function of narrational adjudicator throughout his experience with the "queer old josser" and with Mahony. He readily admits to being "agitated" (En 18) and that his "heart was beating quickly with fear" (En 28), but never indicates what it is that he understands about the man he encountered, whether the nature of the threat was in any way comprehensible to him. Instead, he deflects any actual confrontation with the core situation by measuring his own superiority over Mahony, an advantage that fades under stress: the doltish Mahony proves more resilient to the threat and more than adequate in providing support. Recognizing his scheme to disguise their identities as a "paltry stratagem", the protagonist turns his fears against himself in self-accusation, in an anticipation of his "successor" in "Araby":

> My voice had an accent of forced bravery in it and I was ashamed of my paltry stratagem. I had to call the name again before Mahony saw me and hallooed in answer. How my heart

beat as he came running across the field to me! He ran as if to bring me aid. And I was penitent; for in my heart I had always despised him a little.   (En 28)

The surface problem is allowed to pass unresolved, but an underlying irritant of snobbery has obliquely surfaced instead, consuming the space left vacant. By contrast, the tyranny of silence in the torpor-dominated death room leaves open the possibility that the boy may either have lost faith in the sadly diminished mentor or strengthened his resolve against the petty calumny of the priest's sister. Silence, however, masks a dismay or disappointment in either case. Positing the continuous development of a single protagonist in the childhood stories, and assuming a continuity of sequential time bridging the narratives, a balance sheet can be drawn up: absence of direct parental love, mistrust of human involvements, suspicion regarding the efficacy of a religious vocation, the dead-ending of adventurous quests, the discrediting of chivalric ideals, disappointment in love, and introspective distrust of one's own motives – enough cause cumulatively for the implosion of "anguish and anger" and the self-accusation of "vanity".

THE PRECARIOUS PEDESTAL

There is nothing to prepare the reader of *Dubliners* for the ravine that separates "Araby" from "Eveline", not only because the narrative method shifts from first-person to third, or that childhood disappears into the adult world, but because the continuity of the male child protagonist is disrupted with the new focus on a nineteen-year-old woman. The "Eveline" title leaves little doubt as to the precise focus of the new story, and male continuity, suddenly truncated, goes underground, until the three introductory stories can eventually be re-evaluated as the buried exposition for subsequent narratives of a succession of adult males. Eveline Hill, alternatively, can then be viewed as an originating condition for the Maria in "Clay", despite the calculated separation of the two characters distinctly individuated by name. So sparse is the texture of "Eveline" that controversy over the "sincerity" of her sailor-suitor Frank (and his frank intentions) have occasionally over-shadowed the focal situation of Eveline herself, transforming her into a pawn manipulated either by a male seducer or a male pro-

tector. Yet Eveline, like Maria, is inextricably bound by the constraints of her own condition.

The image of Eveline as arrested in frozen stasis, "passive, like a
helpless animal" in the closing moments of the story (Ev 41), is
more than prepared for in the longer opening scene, where she sits
"at the window watching the evening invade the avenue" (Ev 36) –
the evening actively *invades* while she passively watches. She
breathes in "the odour of dusty cretonne" (Ev 36), wonders "where
on earth all the dust came from" (despite her active efforts – "she
had dusted once a week for so many years" – Ev 37), and just as she
is about to stand up to leave she inhales "the odour of dusty
cretonne" once again (Ev 39). The repetitions that bracket her
experience, that set the boundaries for what is intended as her last
tenure in the house, render it a vacuum of time, a non-experiencing
of time. All of Eveline's "thoughts" are consequently suspect, made
up of gaps and redundancies and contradictions. Having surveyed
a situation in which "she and her brothers and sisters were all
grown up" (Ev 37), she remembers brothers Harry and Ernest (the
latter not only grown up but already dead), yet has no space in her
thoughts for whatever grown-up sisters she may have. She
effectively narrows the perspective so that total dependency is
upon herself, as she conjures up "two young children who had
been left to her charge" (Ev 38) – if *all* of her siblings are grown up,
where do these two young children come from? Maria is only
slightly less vague in her relationship to her two charges in the
enigmatically phrased recollection:

> Joe was a good fellow. She had nursed him and Alphy too; and
> Joe used often say:
>   – Mamma is mamma but Maria is my proper mother.   (Cl 100)

The absence of a surname for Maria leaves a space that "Donnelly"
could conceivably fill, although it need not, and even if assumed,
her exact relationship to her two charges remains problematic.
Maria carries the burden of familial relationships without the
concomitant advantages usually assumed, trapped within a family
circle that is now a blank and may eventually prove a confinement.

In the blank framed by the "odour of dusty cretonne" Eveline
attempts to set the tone of her "irreversible" decision to leave, as
she rationalizes somewhat haughtily: "Of course she had to work

hard both in the house and at business" (Ev 37). The exalted situation (*at business*) is undercut by her depiction of her job as a sales attendant at the Stores, where the voice of Miss Gavan nudging her into performing her work belies her claim to *work hard*, while the slighting reference to *the house* attempts to cancel out her earlier exclamation of "Home!" and her rehearsal of nostalgic regret: "Perhaps she would never see again those familiar objects from which she had never dreamed of being divided" (Ev 37). The newly projected home in Buenos Ayres ("her new home" – Ev 37) replaces the abandoned home that had been reduced to *the house*, a shift conditioned by Eveline's fears of replicating her mother's life in that house. In her new home she "would not be treated as her mother had been" (Ev 37).

Torn between her promise to her dying mother "to keep the home together" and her apprehensions regarding her mother's death ("the pitiful vision of her mother's life laid its spell on the very quick of her being – that life of commonplace sacrifices closing in final craziness" – Ev 40), Eveline assumes that she has opted for escape. Yet at the age of nineteen Eveline Hill may well be repeating her mother's demise with uncanny sameness. Already her father's violence is blamed for having "given her the palpitations" (Ev 38), and in running away from her fate she runs directly into it. At the North Wall docks she stands petrified, "All the seas of the world tumbled about her heart. . . . Amid the seas she sent a cry of anguish" (Ev 41). She too has evolved from *commonplace sacrifices* to a *final craziness*: "She set her white face to him, passive, like a helpless animal. Her eyes gave him no sign of love or farewell or recognition" (Ev 41). Her anguish parallels the suffocation in her heart: *anguish* and *angina* as linguistic doublets.

The suggested extension of young Eveline's life into that of the ageing Maria, assuming that she has been catapulted back from the docks into a continued place in her father's house, both completes and negates a narrative pattern. Spinsterhood, servitude and a limited existence are potentially established for her, and – once the family life breaks up – loneliness as well. The retreat into religion presents another bind as Eveline acknowledges "the promises made to Blessed Margaret Mary Alacoque" on the wall (Ev 37); Maria of course is a devout communicant, although to her discomfort the walls of her "sanctuary" are Protestant: "There was one thing she didn't like and that was the tracts on the walls" (Cl 100).

Eveline has aspired to something that would spare her from "hard work – a hard life" (Ev 38), especially "her mother's life" (Ev 40), and yearned for something better from Frank: "He would give her life, perhaps love, too. But she wanted to live" (Ev 40).

Maria has long since made her adjustment: "After the break-up at home the boys had got her that position in the *Dublin by Lamplight* laundry" and "she had become accustomed to the life of the laundry", even finding the Protestants "very nice people to live with" (Cl 100). And from the laundry, where she keeps her kitchen "spick and span" (Cl 99) – in contrast to Eveline's fruitless dusting – Maria ventures forth on All Hallow's Eve, in greater anticipation of a few hours' respite than Eveline exhibits for a permanent escape: "Maria looked forward to her evening out", for which permission had to be granted ("The matron had given her leave to go out" – Cl 99). She navigates the treacherous Dublin territory with precision and experience, selecting the proper shops, changing trams, and so on – despite weather, ungracious young men and snooty shop assistants. Eveline's anguish (etymologically a *narrowing*) seems unrelated to the naive Maria, although her life is certainly narrow. Her equanimity in dealing with her narrowing existence to date would almost be enviable, were it not that the tiny area of her narrowed life proves to be, at the culmination of the events in "Clay", under siege by infirmity and impending death.

Pathos has the unnerving characteristic of raising hopes that are doomed to be dashed, and the intrusion of Frank into Eveline's life raises unrealizable hopes for her. Whether Frank is a seducer or saviour becomes a moot consideration once the "paralyzed" Eveline removes herself from either seduction or salvation. Exonerating him as legitimately "kind, manly, open-hearted" (Ev 38) or validating his pernicious intent may depend on the accuracy of received information in the text, whether Eveline merely assumes that "Their passage had been booked" (Ev 40) all the way to Buenos Ayres or whether she has actually seen evidence of the full booking. Perhaps the Eveline–Frank relationship has its validation in a previous text, where it appears to have its points of departure: the relationship of Desdemona and Othello. Obviously Mr Hill shares Brabantio's disdain for foreigners (ironically toward "Damned Italians! coming over here"– Ev 40), and his attitude toward the marauding suitor is unequivocal: he "had found out the affair and had forbidden her to have anything to say to him"

(Ev 39) – and Eveline is eventually rendered silent in her final encounter with Frank.

Mr Hill's insistence ("I know these sailor chaps" – Ev 39) parallels that of Brabantio, who *knows* that Othello must have used spells and drugs to entice his daughter, but from Eveline's perspective an attraction to her sailor love is phrased in an echo from Othello's speech of self-justification:

> First of all it had been an excitement for her to have a fellow and then she had begun to like him. He had tales of distant countries. He had started as a deck boy at a pound a month on a ship of the Allan Line going out to Canada. He told her the names of the ships he had been on and the names of the different services. He had sailed through the Straits of Magellan and he told her stories of the terrible Patagonians.   (Ev 39)

In his own voice Othello tells a similar tale:

> Her father loved me, oft invited me,
> Still questioned me the story of my life
> From year to year, the battles, sieges, fortunes,
> That I have passed.
> I ran it through, even from my boyish days
> To the very moment that he bade me tell it.
> Wherein I spake of most disastrous chances,
> Of moving accidents by flood and field,
> Of hairbreadth 'scapes i' the imminent deadly breach,
> Of being taken by the insolent foe
> And sold to slavery, of my redemption thence,
> And portance in my travels' history.
> Wherein of antres vast and deserts idle,
> Rough quarries, rocks, and hills whose heads touch heaven,
> It was my hint to speak – such was the process.
> And of cannibals that each other eat,
> The anthropophagi, and men whose heads
> Do grow beneath their shoulders.
> (Shakespeare, *Othello*, I. iii. 127–45)

Needless to add, he indicates Desdemona's appreciation of his narratives ("She loved me for the dangers I had passed"), and

Frank's watered-down versions of high adventure apparently impressed Eveline as well. It is in vain that one may wish that he had never added that he "had fallen on his feet in Buenos Ayres . . . and had come over to the old country just for a holiday" (Ev 39).

For good or ill Frank has temporarily translated Eveline from her accustomed environment (her mother's death had sold her into slavery and he was presumably assuring her redemption), transforming her name to one of his own fashioning. Bound as she is by her father's surname, marriage would change it to his, but in the interim Frank makes other changes. Banned from her father's house he none the less "used to meet her outside the Stores every evening", and when he "took her to see *The Bohemian Girl* . . . she felt elated as she sat in an unaccustomed part of the theatre with him" (Ev 39). That he "used to call her Poppens out of fun" (Ev 39) establishes certain proprietory rights (possessing by renaming), yet at the moment of crisis, when he realizes that she is holding back and not accompanying him on board the ship, he reverts to her traditional name: "Eveline! Evvy!" (Ev 41), rather than Poppens. Eveline has never actually been "the lass that loves a sailor", despite Frank's singing of the song that made her feel "pleasantly confused" (Ev 39), and only temporarily was she ever Poppens. The weeks with Frank were a theatrical diversion, an acting out of *The Bohemian Girl*, with Eveline out of her milieu, *in an accustomed part of the theatre*. To conjecture that she will have a middle-aged existence similar to that of Maria is to credit her with having a future at all: at the end of "Eveline" she stands totally inert, a nineteen-year-old with an astonished heart. Her narrative resembles that of the three childhood stories to which it naturally belongs, tales of a child's life up to the moment of traumatic closure. In none of the succeeding stories of *Dubliners* is childhood recapitulated as in these four opening narratives.

"A DEDALE OF LUSTY YOUTH"

A space of seven years separates Eveline Hill from the youngest of the "youths" who populate the next three tales, bracketing her between three male children and the young adult males. The link with Jimmy Doyle is at first an ironic one: whereas Eveline is bound within two framing traps, her dustladen home and the confining barrier at the North Wall, Jimmy is seen in a car "scudding in towards Dublin . . . careering homeward" (Af 42), although his eventual "entrapment" at daybreak on board the yacht will identify him irrevocably with her. Almost totally free of any bonds the footloose Lenehan will traverse the streets of Dublin in unbounded freedom, except as he realizes himself bound by his poverty and unconsciously walking in consistently constricting concentric circles. "The Boarding House" will then present Bob Doran within the Mooney domain, more and more aware of himself as a "helpless animal", unable to "ascend through the roof and fly away to another country" (Bo 67–8), while the closing scene of Polly in Bob's room reveals her to be trapped as well. The narrational introductions to Doyle, Lenehan and Doran establish them sub-liminally but immediately in terms of their distinctive dis-advantages, primarily in their bonds to their "antagonists", although the narrative method of the disadvantaging of each of them varies in each introduction.

In "After the Race" the pecking order of status is apparent, even blatant, prefaced by a deceptive differentiation that at first seems inapplicable to the participants: that "through this channel of poverty and inaction the Continent sped its wealth and industry" (Af 42) separates the setting of Irish deprivation from the four "hilarious" young men in the Continental automobile. The cata-loguing of the four, however, arrives at last at the least important, the Irish "intruder" in his native city: "They were Charles Ségouin, the owner of the car; André Rivière, a young electrician of Canadian birth; a huge Hungarian named Villona and a neatly groomed young man named Doyle" (Af 42–3). Doyle will soon acquire a given name, but in this initial context he is outside the league that includes Charles Ségouin and André Rivière, and in the company of Villona, who will be identified as "a brilliant pianist – but, unfortunately, very poor" (Af 44) – by contrast, Doyle has a "fortune" to invest. French, Canadian, Hungarian, Irish: Canada as a colony, its French-speaking populace second-class citizens; Hungary as a junior "partner" in an Austro-Hungarian Empire dominated by Vienna, as Ireland is a vassal state in the British Empire ruled from London. The "entertaining" Villona feeds his huge appetite at the expense of his hosts, playing the piano for them but abstaining from the gaming table. Jimmy Doyle, on the other hand, proves to be one of the two "heaviest" losers at cards (Af 48): his position in the back seat of the car with Villona should have been indicative of his "place".

The swath that their car cuts through Irish poverty and inaction suggests a calculated scheme to fleece the inexperienced Jimmy Doyle, to put him in a bind, yet it would require a careful observer to spot the manipulation of the shell game that victimizes him. If it really is some sort of confidence game, it depends on the gullibility of the victim, yet Jimmy's business-wise father supports the idea of investing in Ségouin's motoring interests – but he may well have miscalculated the character of his son:

> Of course, the investment was a good one and Ségouin had managed to give the impression that it was by a favour of friendship the mite of Irish money was to be included in the capital of the concern. Jimmy had a respect for his father's shrewdness in business matters and in this case it had been his father who had first suggested the investment; money to be made in the motor business, pots of money.   (Af 44–5)

It may also have been the senior Doyle who was out of his element in this case, bound by his own greed: the language of "money to be made" sounds as if it is his.

Investing in a business and gambling at cards are paralleled and opposed to each other in the course of the narrative (*pots of money* in terms of the former suggests the latter). The card game appears to have developed spontaneously and depends for its inception on several accidentals: the meeting of Ségouin and his Cambridge friend Routh and the meeting of Rivière with his friend Farley, the latter providing his yacht as venue, but himself a heavy loser (presumably). The call for "Cards! cards!" (Af 48) remains un-identified, a narrative ploy that replicates the calculated ploy of a card-sharp in masking his identity as the instigator of the game. Villona wisely plays the piano instead; Rivière "disappears" from serious contention when it becomes apparent that "the game lay between Routh and Ségouin" – and "Routh won" (Af 48). Whether Jimmy Doyle has been purposely set up, or even whether the scheme to "take" Doyle one way or the other has been undercut by the intrusive Englishman, Jimmy is a gullible contributor to his own demise.

Just as Jimmy Doyle "trails" into the events of "After the Race", so does Lenehan appear as the last item even in a list of two, as is immediately predicated in the introduction of the pair in "Two Gallants" (bound by his inferior position he is shunted out of bounds by Corley):

> Two young men came down the hill of Rutland Square. One of them was just bringing a long monologue to a close. The other, who walked on the verge of the path and was at times obliged to step on to the road, owing to his companion's rudeness, wore an amused listening face. (Tw 49)

By analogy the tale itself is a long monologue on the verge of being brought to a close, and the teetering Lenehan rudely forced into a marginalized role in a narrative in which he is the protagonist.

The tension in "Two Gallants" depends on the vacillation between active and passive roles, the decision predetermined by the gambit of their initial appearances. Lenehan is prevented from putting together a concerted attack (by his "poverty and inaction"), and is described as seriously divided against himself: "His breeches, his white rubber shoes and his jauntily slung waterproof expressed youth. But his figure fell into rotundity at the waist [the Rutland Square opening locates him at the Rotunda], his hair was scant and grey and his face, when the waves of expression had passed over it, had a ravaged look" (Tw 50). The operative article of Lenehan's attire is that tell-tale raincoat, which he "slung over one shoulder in toreador fashion" (Tw 50). An overweight, overaged torero ("He would be thirty-one in November" – Tw 58), he lacks the control of his immediate terrain, the bull-like Corley constantly edging him out of contention. Lenehan instinctively knows what every practising bullfighter must learn, to select his own *querencia*, the part of the arena in which the bull is least comfortable, where the bull cannot exert control: contesting within the bull's *querencia* is risky and only for the bravest of toreros. ("Are you trying to get inside me?" (Tw 54), Corley asks with annoyance when Lenehan wants to get a look at the slavey.) In Corley's absence the "unbounded" Lenehan has all of Dublin as his undisputed world as he *circles* his immediate environs of the city centre, but when he ventures into a "poor-looking shop" for a meagre meal (Tw 57), he is confronted by suspicion from the other customers – he is trespassing, very much out-of-bounds, in an *unaccustomed part of the theatre*.

The moment of truth comes with his eventual re-engagement with Corley, but as he runs toward him, "Anxiety and his swift run made him pant"(Tw 60). He had worried that Corley had "given him the slip" (Tw 59), and in sighting him at last he moves in for his share of the spoils: "Lenehan ran after him, settling the waterproof on his shoulders with one hand" (Tw 60). His active participation, his meanderings and schemings, keeping his eye always on the main chance, his panting pursuit of his goal result in his being there to partake in the benefits of Corley's "small gold coin". But the triumph is strictly Corley's, reducing Lenehan to marginality, outside the Pale; he never stopped skirting the verge, passively humiliating himself before the victor: "with a grave gesture, [Corley] extended a hand towards the light and, smiling, opened it slowly to the gaze of his disciple" (Tw 60). All of Lenehan's activity throughout the tale has brought him from his initial discipleship to his ultimate discipleship, his evening a static vacuum not unlike Eveline's.

The Bob Doran who is at the centre of "The Boarding House" is as much the prisoner of his own condition as he is the figure contained in, trapped in the titular domain, a *querencia* that belongs to the Mooneys, in which he is totally unable to manoeuvre. He spends the Sunday morning within the walls of his room in the house, a caged animal that will only be released when it is time for him to enter the arena to confront the gladiatorial presence of Mrs Mooney. To reach Bob Doran the reader must first pass through every other significant character of the narrative, the members of the Mooney family that collectively team up to enclose him in bondage. First, there is the Madam herself, "a woman who was quite able to keep things to herself: a determined woman" (Bo 61). Second, there is her son, "who had the reputation of being a hard case" (Bo 62). Third, there is Polly Mooney, "a slim girl of nineteen . . . a little perverse madonna" (Bo 62–3). That the Mooney siblings are listed as "the Madam's son" and "the Madam's daughter" (Bo 62) indicates who rules the roost and the reliability of the support team, and the Madam's weapon is also specified: "She dealt with moral problems as a cleaver deals with meat" (Bo 63). More than halfway through the story of Bob Doran, Doran himself is at last "discovered" in his den – the last item in the series.

Whereas Jimmy Doyle and Lenehan actually imagined themselves in motion, motorized and ambulatory respectively, they too were fixed within the paralytic confines of their Dublin, their "activities" in the ultimate boundaries of the Naas Road to Kingstown, Rutland Square to Ely Place, merely illusory. Doran, however, exists in literal entrapment, without the illusion of escape that temporarily let Eveline get as far at the North Wall docks. (The nineteen-year-old Polly parallels the nineteen-year-old Eveline, with Bob as her seducer and saviour, although there is no indication that she views him as "very kind, manly, open-hearted".) Doran's room is a replica of Eveline's dusty parlour, but whereas she longs to run away and marry, he is caught in the non-existence of a choice: to "marry her or run away" (Bo 65). Eveline had for a while placed her hopes in Buenos Ayres, far beyond the boundaries of Dublin, but with far fewer self-illusions Bob was hardly vouchsafed even a glimpse of a promised land, "another country where he would never hear again of his trouble" (Bo 67–8).

Doran's plight begins where those of others had concluded: at the end of "Araby" the boy's "eyes burned with anguish and anger" (Ar 35); at the end of "Eveline" her "eyes gave . . . no sign of love or farewell or recognition" (Ev 41); at the beginning of Doran's scene in "The Boarding House" his eyes are already affected: "every two or three minutes a mist gathered on his glasses so that he had to take them off and polish them with his pocket-handkerchief" (Bo 65). When he finally leaves his room the same gesture closes the scene, fencing him in as the dusty cretonne curtains had framed Eveline's scene in her parlour: "his glasses became so dimmed with moisture that he had to take them off and polish them" (Bo 67). Doran then runs a reverse gauntlet of the Mooney opposition: first, Polly invades his room, effectively softening him up for her mother's call, like a priest visiting the condemned prisoner's cell; then he encounters Jack Mooney on the stairs, his warder; and finally the Madam, his executioner. Almost in a parody of his blind entrapment, "Polly sat for a little time on the side of the bed, crying. Then she dried her eyes and went over to the looking-glass. She dipped the end of the towel in the water-jug and refreshed her eyes with the cool water" (Bo 68).

Doyle's rites of passage take him by automobile, on foot, on a "car", by train, by rowboat on a lateral trek that slashes across the Dublin cityscape (the Naas Road, Dame Street, Grafton Street,

St Stephen's Green, Westland Row, Kingstown Station: "Rapid motion through space" – Af 44). Lenehan's aimless peregrinations (Rutland Square, Nassau Street, Kildare Street, Hume Street, Merrion Square, St Stephen's Green, Grafton Street, Rutland Square, Capel Street, Dame Street, George's Street, Grafton Street, St Stephen's Green, Merrion Street, Baggot Street, St Stephen's Green, Ely Place: "He was tired of knocking about" – Tw 57) also gave the illusion of movement, yet their final tightening circularity restricts them to futile stasis (although Zeno's arrow can also be located at each juncture in space, it never reaches a destination). Only by the contrast of illusory motion do Doyle and Lenehan achieve anything more than the confined Eveline Hill or Bob Doran: the shadows of the cave wall play out the lives of these shut-ins of Dublin.

What functions in these stories of childhood and young adulthood carries over as well as into the stories of maturity and public life. The spaces and distances that set the boundaries between individual tales are narrowed and bridged by the same elements that give each its distinct individuality, and the autonomy of the individual characters is often problematic, their situations equivocal, their destinies indefinite. As isolate Dubliners they share a common environment, bounded in a nutshell of infinite space, but also share common characteristics, not the least of which is a limited pool of common names (like Jack and James and Tom). The often acknowledged style of "scrupulous meanness" affects the economical use of nomenclature and of language, "mean" in its controlled miserliness but also in bringing diverse creations toward an operative mean, or norm or bind, a limited sampling from the strand of "average" life in Dublin. As people they are as interrelated as vocabulary, of words that share a common etymology, similar roots, double existences, cognate developments along individuated paths from a root source. The designation of "paralysis" in the formative phase of the development of the *Dubliners* narratives establishes an originating concept that reappears in the confluences of *Angst*, anxiety, angina, anguish, with their intersecting connotations of strangulation, suffocation, narrowing, constricting, binding. Gazing into the eyes of these carriers of the communal condition, we see into their confines and confinements and see each of them reflected in the eyes of the others.

6
Duplicitous Bonds: Talents of Maturity

"O God, I could be bounded in a nutshell and count myself a king of infinite space, were it not that I have bad dreams."

Hamlet, II. ii.

"If it be now, 'tis not to come; if it be not to come, it will be now; if it not be now, yet it will come . . . "

Hamlet, V. ii.

The constraints of childhood are assumed to be the obvious ones of an incomplete being not yet ready for the world outside, protected and even secured within necessary confines: the boy in "The Sisters" is allowed to navigate the distance between his own home and that of Father Flynn; the boy in "An Encounter" that between home and school (which he violates by an unlicensed excursion in the direction of the Pigeon House); the boy in "Araby" permitted, with misgivings, the nocturnal venture to the bazaar. The liberties allowed the young adolescent extend the boundaries and remove various barriers, yet Eveline Hill is constrained by the limitations of the straight line between home and "the Stores", usurping for herself the prohibited escapes with Frank that take her as far as the theatre, and the North Wall docks, until she is pulled back. The strictures imposed by her father, her dead mother and Margaret Mary Alacoque prove to be greater than the freedom she associates with the sailor and the seas that extend outward from restrictive Dublin: as a woman she has fewer territorial rights than the male "child" of "Araby".

Joyce pushes the ultimate limits of the Roman *adolescentia* to include Lenehan and Doran as well as Jimmy Doyle, the men in their early thirties arrested short of adult maturity by economic restraints inexorably imposed upon them. Lenehan has presumably made the choice of a carefree existence that makes the streets of Dublin unboundedly available to him, but his impoverished circumstances make them his prison-without-walls instead. Bob Doran has chosen responsible employment, with as few personal attachments as the unmarried Lenehan, yet the very job that gives him his security and independence becomes the rope that reins him in. It is true that Jimmy Doyle has no Catholic wine merchant to regulate his affairs, no landlady standing over him with a cleaver, no need to depend on his wits in order to cadge free drinks, but he is as vulnerable outside his limited domain as the others, blinded by the freedom that his access to money suggests, and eventually as victimized by the suave Ségouin as Lenehan is by the coarse Corley. If Eveline's cloistered timidity pulls her up short at the sight of the ship in Dublin Harbour, Jimmy's temerity propels him out to the yacht that holds the means of his self-destruction.

The expansion that marks the differentiation between childhood and adolescence is illusive for all four of these "adolescents", each of whom is inexorably claimed by tight, confining spaces in varying forms: Eveline balks at confinement on board ship but has taken with her to the docks the confinement of the house she had hoped to abandon; Jimmy Doyle feels totally unconfined in the speeding car, but its ultimate destination is the gambling ship of perpetual night; Lenehan attempts to stay outside walled boxes, and is even weary of pubs, but the need for food brings into the "Refreshment Bar" that is alien territory for him, and escape from there only lands him in Corley's hands; Bob Doran has "invaded" Polly Mooney's space, and for his transgression has had his sanctuary metamorphose into his prison, with Polly now in possession there as well. James Duffy, however, has never allowed a Polly Mooney into his life, and as a man of maturity he seems to have the freedom that only a hermit in self-defined confinement can attain.

"IN CELIBATE MATRIMONY"

Duffy's shadowy precursor is the misogynistic St Kevin of Glendalough. Like the saint who had retreated from the decadent society of pagan Dublin to an isolated existence among the lakes in the Wicklow Hills, Duffy chose the unpretentious suburb of

Chapelizod because he "wished to live as far as possible from the city of which he was a citizen" (Pa 107), and had a similar disdain for "an obtuse middle class that entrusted its morality to policemen and its fine arts to impresarios" (Pa 111). His asceticism is barely disguised by his proper clothes and his responsible position in a commercial bank, but his solitary life is none the less monkish: "an old sombre house" and an "uncarpeted room . . . free from pictures" (Pa 107), and every item of furniture of his own choosing. Just as St Kevin carved out a dwelling for himself from the Glendalough woods (a hollow tree trunk by day and a cave by night), Duffy has his "shelves of white wood", his "new cedarwood pencils", and carries a "stout hazel" walking-stick (Pa 107, 108). He gravitates between home and work: "every morning he went into the city by tram and every evening walked home from the city" (Pa 112). His particular version of the mortification of the flesh consists not only of "living at a little distance from his body" (Pa 108), but also in the simple meals of "a bottle of lager beer and a small trayful of arrowroot biscuits" for lunch (Pa 108) and a dinner menu of a "certain plain honesty in the bill of fare" (Pa 109).

Duffy's life is an updated version of that of the seventh-century eremite-saint, as he lives "his spiritual life without any communion with others" and avoids "the society of Dublin's gilded youth", having "neither companions nor friends" (Pa 109). Even his physical appearance suggests these reclusish aspects ("A mediaeval doctor would have called him saturnine. His face, which carried the entire tale of his years, was of the brown tint of Dublin streets. On his long and rather harsh head grew dry black hair and a tawny moustache did not quite cover an unamiable mouth. His cheekbones also gave his face a harsh character" – Pa 108). None the less, with all these facets of protective covering, James Duffy remains vulnerable. His is a spiritual quest that seems primarily turned inward, but the ideal of that quest may be a madonna figure that he has steeled himself from anticipating. When Emily Sinico "intrudes" into his privacy, Duffy is quick to respond: "He took the remark as an invitation to talk" (Pa 109), yet is so suspicious of any such intrusion that he waits until the third accidental meeting with her to accept the validity of her intercession. And once the relationship develops he insists on moving it to her space, to "her little cottage outside Dublin" (Pa 111), to assure himself that their intimacy was regarded with absolute favour. All of his responses are essentially transcendental: "Her companionship was like a warm soil about an exotic"; "The dark discreet room, their isolation, the music that still vibrated in their ears united them"; "This union exalted him"; "He thought that in her eyes he would ascend to an angelic stature" (Pa 111). The sacred and the profane have an uncanny way of resembling each other, and the "dark discreet room" is as much brothel as it is sanctuary; the "soul's incurable loneliness" (Pa 111) narrows the space for someone who lives at a "little distance from his body." What Mrs Sinico detected in Mr Duffy was already there in his eyes, which "gave the impression of a man ever alert to greet a redeeming instinct in others but often disappointed" (Pa 108).

Although contemptuous of and withdrawn from that "obtuse middle class", Duffy, by his withdrawal and disguise, never allows himself to cross over the boundary beyond respectability. His secret plan to steal from his bank is self-indulgent fantasy, since he knows that no real opportunity will ever arise and he certainly never intends taking any sort of risk. His attendance at Socialist meetings is equally secretive, and the obtuseness of the working class parallels for him that of his own class, so he can grant himself the licence to withdraw from that as well. When Emily Sinico crosses the line from spiritual union to clutching "his hand passionately" (Pa 111), she unwittingly invites the same violent response that Katherine received from the saintly Kevin, who hurls her into the lake where she drowns. Without the saint's total absorption in his spirituality Duffy eventually becomes aware of his guilt: "Why had he sentenced her to death?" he asks himself, belatedly acknowledging that "One human being had seemed to love him and he had denied her life and happiness: he had sentenced her to ignominy, a death of shame" (Pa 117). But Duffy had already answered his question as to why he rejected her love: middle-class propriety had insisted upon it ("He could not have carried on a comedy of deception with her; he could not have lived with her openly" – Pa 116). Duffy had bound himself within the strictly circumscribed space of bourgeois morality despite his aloof demeanour and his silently proclaimed *non serviam*: his repressed self is revealed surreptitiously when he reads the newspaper account of Mrs Sinico's death, "moving his lips as a priest does when he reads the prayers *Secreto*" (Pa 113).

What Duffy reads is a clinically impassive account of the "DEATH OF A LADY AT SYDNEY PARADE" (Pa 113), and the bond that had existed for him with that lady changes the relationship between him and the newspaper that he read every evening "for dessert" at the George's Street restaurant (Pa 112). The subheading, "A PAINFUL CASE", reflects back on himself once he has read and re-read the story, so that the bond with Emily Sinico maintains itself with tenacity once he realizes himself complicit in her death. Journalistic discretion exceeds its mandate at the summation of the story, when the findings of the inquest ("The jury returned a verdict in accordance with the medical evidence and exonerated Lennon [the engine-driver] from all blame" – Pa 115) never indicate whether her death was suicide or accident. The medical examiner himself was indecisive, on one hand disallowing a mere accident but unwilling to commit himself on suicidal method: "The injuries were not sufficient to have caused death in a normal person. Death, in his opinion, had been probably due to shock and sudden failure of the heart's action" (Pa 114), so that the dual determinants of anguish and angina again appear operative. The cause of death, however, is obliquely insinuated in another kind of testimony, one that is reiterated by the journalist, the railway porter and the emissary from the railway company, as if mesmerized by a phrase that seems self-evident but remains elliptical: "while attempting to cross the line" (Pa 113), "observed a woman attempting to cross the lines" (Pa 114), "in the habit of crossing the lines late at night" (Pa 114). Emily Sinico had transgressed four years before, inviting James Duffy by a grasping of hands to cross the line as well. But Duffy, who, although he visited "his relatives at Christmas" and escorted them "to the cemetery when they died", "conceded nothing further to the conventions which regulate the civil life" (Pa 109), and although he had spoken to Mrs Sinico "of what he held sacred" (Pa 115), he conceded nothing further along those lines either.

Had they not lived in such separate universes Duffy and Chandler might have passed each other in the streets of Dublin, Duffy walking home from the restaurant in George's Street just as Chandler was heading toward Corless's to meet Ignatius Gallaher. The message that might have passed telepathetically from Duffy to Chandler would have been that "every bond . . . is a bond to sorrow" (Pa 112), but it would have fallen on unresponsive ears since "Little Chandler's thoughts ever since lunch-time had been of his meeting with Gallaher" (Li 70), perhaps to be remembered later that evening. Like "Two Gallants", "A Little Cloud" is a tale about male bonding, and like its predecessor a rather perverse tale in which the bonds are, if not of sorrow, at least of disappointment.

Corley had set his tame playmate free for the evening to entertain himself as best he could, knowing that he held in his hands the reins with which to draw him in, and only when (as on 16 June 1904) Corley is devoid of small gold coins did the worm turn against him: "he had a row with Lenehan and called him to Stephen a mean bloody swab with a sprinkling of a number of other uncalledfor expressions" (Eu 146–8). The eight-year hiatus in the Little Chandler–Great Gallaher "friendship" has resulted in a loosening of the bonds that had once held them together, but at this resumption of their relationship Chandler is in no way dependent on his more successful counterpart and appreciates that he is bound for Corless's in response to "Gallaher's invitation" (Li 70). Exuding a newfound self-confidence, almost Duffy-like in feeling himself "superior to the people he passed", as "his soul revolted against the dull inelegance of Capel Street" (Li 73), he heads straight for the arena in which Gallaher has his strength, his *querencia*. But timid Chandler already has a history of seeking danger by occasionally crossing the line into *terra incognita*:

> It was his habit to walk swiftly in the street even by day and whenever he found himself in the city late at night he hurried on his way apprehensively and excitedly. Sometimes, however, he courted the causes of his fear. He chose the darkest and narrowest streets and, as he walked boldly forward, the silence that was spread about his footsteps troubled him, and the wandering silent figures troubled him; and at times a sound of low fugitive laughter made him tremble like a leaf.   (Li 72)

Just as Eveline had hoped to use Frank as her means of escape, Chandler tried his hand at manipulating the "low fugitive" Gallaher. Having been the one who "Eight years before . . . had seen his friend off at the North Wall and wished him godspeed" (Li 70), he interprets Gallaher's return to Dublin as somehow to be turned to his own advantage ("He wondered whether he could write a poem to express his idea. Perhaps Gallaher might be able to get it into some London paper for him" – Li 73). (There is no indication that his "meeting with Gallaher" was anything but accidental, that Gallaher in anyway sought out Chandler on his return to Dublin.) In effect, Chandler conjures up his own Ignatius Gallaher, a precursor in his escape from Dublin that Chandler might now follow, a model that he could improve upon, a totem figure that he could destroy and replace – it might even be surmised that in his heart he "had always despised him a little". The Gallaher that he imagines for his own purposes is shot through with contradictions, the "travelled air", the "well-cut tweed suit", and the "fearless accent" (Li 70) now impress Chandler in his re-encounter with him, but the Gallaher of eight years ago "was wild", and mixed with "a rakish set of fellows", "drank freely and borrowed money on all sides" (Li 72). Chandler now recalls these characteristics with begrudging respect and even admiration, yet they had led to the inescapable transgression that the moral Chandler tries to pass off lightly: "In the end he had got mixed up in some shady affair, some money transaction: at least, that was one version of his flight" (Li 72). Chandler prefers to write his own version of various aspects of Ignatius Gallaher, especially the version that would fit his own flight. There is no evidence from the single-focused recollection that Chandler was the *only* friend to see Gallaher off at the North Wall docks, but that self-sustained image can then translate itself to a reversal of roles: for the course of his hour or so with Gallaher in Corless's he makes an abortive effort to take on Gallaher's guise and effect his own escape. Even when the reunion has soured and Chandler is fully aware of his friend's condescension, his retort is to put Gallaher in his shoes, saddle him with a pretty-faced Annie: "You'll put your head in the sack, repeated Little Chandler stoutly, like everyone else if you can find the girl" (Li 81). When that happens, Chandler (in a "well-cut tweed suit") will be on board ship for London.

The Gallaher that Little Chandler constructs for himself will be deconstructed by Ignatius Gallaher himself from his vantage point at Corless's bar, revealing himself as a creature of contradictions that he is constantly attempting to reconcile. Whereas Chandler had assured himself that "Gallaher had got on", and that he "had become a brilliant figure on the London Press" (Li 70, 71), Gallaher grumbles about "Press life": "It pulls you down" (Li 75). Chandler even credits the old Gallaher of Dublin days with "many signs of future greatness", an attribution that he makes belatedly, insisting that "nobody denied him talent" (Li 72). But Gallaher confesses to an existence that is "Always hurry and scurry, looking for copy and sometimes not finding it: and then, always to have something new in your stuff" (Li 75). His divided self becomes immediately apparent from the conflict between his eyes, "which were of bluish slate-colour", and "the vivid orange tie he wore", characteristics described as "rival features" (Li 75), but reconciled toward the end of the scene at Corless's when "Ignatius Gallaher turned his orange tie and slate-blue eyes full upon his friend" (Li 81). Chandler had sought somehow to divide and conquer, to establish his hegemony over his adversary by manoeuvring him off-balance, but Gallaher is experienced enough in his shiftiness to unite behind an invulnerable façade.

The Gallaher that Chandler had created in his own imagination (just as he had imagined the houses along the Liffey as "a band of tramps, huddled together" – Li 73) quickly disintegrates when directly confronted, and it is a disappointed Chandler who goads "his friend" into betraying the cruder self now hidden beneath the travelled air and well-tailored clothes. But Chandler resists losing his mock-creation completely, rationalizing that the "old personal charm was still there under his new gaudy manner", although he was none the less "beginning to feel somewhat disillusioned. Gallaher's accent and way of expressing himself did not please him. There was something vulgar in his friend which he had not observed before" (Li 76–7). It becomes apparent from his attitude as he approaches the meeting that Chandler is "courting" Gallaher, and his exposure of vulgarity allies him with Bob Doran, who when confronted with the inevitability of marriage with Polly Mooney, chafed at the realization that his friends would detect that she "*was* a little vulgar" (Bo 66). Chandler has come a long way from admiring Gallaher's "fearless accent", but the effect of the whiskies leaves him still confused, "sharing for a brief space Gallaher's vagrant and triumphant life" (Li 80).

Vagrancy and triumph are not necessarily in conflict with each other in Chandler's scale of values: Gallaher's experiences in London and Paris particularly activate Chandler's imagination, despite the persistent awareness that Gallaher has been cast out of Ireland, that he absconded under a cloud (and his friend at the docks was perhaps complicit). For his own vanity Chandler has conjured up a Gallaher deficient in character and integrity in comparison with himself, and therefore those acknowledged worldly successes are viewed as accomplishments that the morally superior Chandler should be able to duplicate, if not surpass. For every quality of brilliance and greatness attributed to the absconder, Chandler yokes a concomitant "shabby and necessitous guise" (Li 71), a gaudy manner, a vagrancy. His presumed emulation of the emigrant journalist masks eight years of harboured

resentment, and he sets up his straw man for a fall, working up
sufficient courage to take on his manufactured Goliath:

> He felt acutely the contrast between his own life and his friend's,
> and it seemed to him unjust. Gallaher was his inferior in birth
> and education. He was sure that he could do something better
> than his friend had ever done, or could ever do, something
> higher than mere tawdry journalism if he only got the chance.
> What was it that stood in his way? His unfortunate timidity! He
> wished to vindicate himself in some way, to assert his manhood.
> He saw behind Gallaher's refusal of his invitation. Gallaher was
> only patronising him by his friendliness just as he was
> patronising Ireland by his visit.   (Li 80)

The various modulations in tone every time the phrase "his friend"
is employed works toward compromising the concept of friendship
now presumably operative in "A Little Cloud", unmasking a
pseudo-Smith to Gallaher's Mahony. That Chandler in his turn is
patronizing Gallaher becomes as evident as his patronizing an
Ireland he also wishes to leave behind: for the approval of the
"English critics" the pseudo-poet adopts *"The Celtic note"* and tries
to twist his name into a version that is "more Irish-looking" (Li 74),
unconsciously envying Ignatius Gallaher's pre-eminently Irish-
looking name.

   Self-profession of timidity locks into place the notion of a
permanently disadvantaged Little Chandler, somewhat stoically
bending under adversity. Yet Chandler so obviously fantasizes a
secret life in which he can substitute a measure of temerity for
timidity, as when he "chose the darkest and narrowest of streets" in
lieu of his usual habit of hurrying "on his way apprehensively and
excitedly" (Li 72). His rashness in bearding Gallaher in his own
den, in entering the bull's *querencia*, takes him into so unaccustomed a part of the theatre as an elegant restaurant ("He had
never been in Corless's but he knew the value of the name" – Li
72). Gallaher was the one who selected the terrain, not an ordinary
pub where his gaudy manner might be more appropriately
accommodated, but a place where he could impress and lord it
over his friend (who is there at Gallaher's invitation); Chandler
attempts to gain an advantage by inviting Gallaher to his place
("My wife will be delighted to meet you. We can have a little music
and – ": Li 79), but Gallaher sidesteps that danger immediately

and without much subtlety. The Dublin stay-at-home overestimates his prowess in his native city, just as he had underestimated the real Gallaher – as differentiated from the one he so conveniently contrived. The jaunty adversary knows the moral force of his opponent ("You're the same serious person that used to lecture me on Sunday mornings" – Li 76), and it is not surprising that when first confronted in his coign of vantage, he was "leaning with his back against the counter and his feet planted far apart" (Li 74), the confident pose of confrontation.

For all his skills in transforming the Dublin cityscape into his own poetic figures, Chandler undervalues the double-edged dangers in his town, although "He picked his way deftly through all that minute vermin-like life and under the shadow of the gaunt spectral mansions in which the old nobility of Dublin had roistered" (Li 71–2). His attempts to imitate the old roisterers had landed Gallaher in trouble and sent him into ignominious exile, but still did not leave the serious, lecturing Chandler in command of the field. On one hand Chandler sets forth this evening to rid Dublin once again of the likes of the roistering Gallaher, while on the other hand he seeks to learn Gallaher's formula for successful escape. Frustrated in either vanquishing his enemy or gleaning his enemy's secret, his only parting volley against "his friend" is to transform him into his own image, the unhappily married man, "wishing long life and happiness to Mr and Mrs Ignatius Gallaher" (Li 81). The unmarried Gallaher instinctively knows what timid Chandler has not yet admitted to himself, and is blunt in declaring an aversion that mirrors the reality of Chandler's home life: "Must get a bit stale, I should think" (Li 82).

Like many of his various predecessors, Chandler eventually bemoans his fate ("He was a prisoner for life" – Li 84). He had escaped from Corless's and is inside the safety of his own home, where he hopes to replace Gallaher with Lord Byron, only to fall victim to the bullying of his wife and the insistent wailing of his child, the hostages to fortune that he had wished on Gallaher. The house should have taken on the protective guise of a sanctuary after the threatening streets and the encounter in Gallaher's haunt, but an angry wife, a bawling child and cumulative frustrations reduce his retreat to an entrapment: "Could he not escape from his little house?" (Li 83). His domain is predicated on inconsistency, as his recapitulation of the incident of Annie and the blouse indicates: at first she accepts the gift with pleasure, kisses him and tells him how "pretty" it is; then she learns the price and is angry with him; and then she tries it on and is delighted with it and kisses him again. An already timid and indecisive Chandler is being reduced to the status of a Pavlovian rodent – and "pretty" emerges as the key term in his ambivalence toward his wife, just as "friend" had taken on an ambiguous tone in his dealings with Gallaher. He looks hard at a photograph of Annie and particularly at her eyes: "Certainly they were pretty and the face itself was pretty. But he found something mean in it" (Li 83).

The gap that separates the "mean" from the "pretty" narrows decidedly, until a comprehensive equation takes shape between them, a balance of interlocked entities in which the masculine pronoun that stands for Chandler vies with the feminine pronoun that designates Annie: "He found something mean in the pretty furniture which *he* had bought for *his* house on the hire system. Annie chose it *herself* and it reminded him of *her*. It too was prim and pretty" (Li 83; emphasis added). When Chandler narrows the focus on Annie's eyes, two opposing sets of values come into perspective, the real and the naively imagined:

> The composure of the eyes irritated him. They repelled him and defied him: there was no passion in them, no rapture. He thought of what Gallaher had said about rich Jewesses. Those dark Oriental eyes, he thought, how full they are of passion, of voluptuous longing! ... Why had he married the eyes in the photograph? (Li 83)

The disintegration of the friendship with Gallaher, based as it was on Chandler's false assumptions and secret scheme, transfers to the relationship with Annie as well, and in the closing moments of "A Little Cloud" he regresses to adolescent self-pity as "tears of remorse started to his eyes" (Li 85). Like the boy in "The Sisters" he is reduced to silence in the wake of the baby's caterwauling and its mother's constant monologue; like the boy in "An Encounter" he is "penitent" regarding the falsity of his capacity for friendship; and like the boy in "Araby" he might well regard himself as "a creature driven and derided by vanity". The Little Chandler who lives in a little house has been dragged regressively into infancy, identified with the crying baby but not the recipient of the mother's cooing words. Annie's basilisk glance has diminished him into nothingness ("Little Chandler sustained for one moment the gaze of her

eyes and his heart closed together as he met the hatred in them" –
Li 85). To Annie it is the infant who is "My little man" (Li 85).

"O LOST, AND BY THE WIND GRIEVED, GHOST . . . "

Along the boundary lines that link Chandler to his normal course
from office to home, the stop at Corless's seems to be only a slight
detour, never to be repeated, and although there is no reason to
assume that his office at the King's Inn does not remain safe
territory, his home now becomes enemy terrain, where his heart is
in danger of "closing together". For Farrington the office is now a
"hornet's nest", where he would be constantly "hounded", and
never allowed "an hour's rest" (Co 92) – and he "loathed returning
to his home" (Co 97). His place of refuge had always been the
public houses, and he gravitates among several of them in a
rotation that should offer him both stasis and energetic movement.
Farrington's desires to "rush out and revel in violence" (Co 90)
signals his readiness for combat, a warrior familiar with the terrain
that he himself circumscribes, his *querencia*, where he is invulnerable as a moving target and always able to assume a protective
covering. Yet his safe space is invaded at every turn, by Higgins
stealing his thunder, by Weathers disarming him in hand-to-hand
combat, and by the woman-in-the-big-hat mocking his impotence.
If the pubs are no longer snug and secure for him, Farrington is a
displaced person, a wanderer like Lenehan, who has no hearth to
return to but had also considered the pubs *terra cognita*, yet now
admits that he hardly looks forward to the usual pub crawl: "He
knew that he would have to speak a great deal, to invent and to
amuse, and his brain and throat were too dry for such a task" – he
feels condemned to "keep on walking" (Tw 56). Another aimless
wanderer is James Duffy, suddenly propelled out of his favourite
eating place by the "Painful Case" article, which he re-reads as
soon as he returns home, only to rush out of his room, first to a
public house and then into Phoenix Park.

The stories of maturity extend the streak of disappointments that
characterized the young Dubliners, concentrating to an even
greater extent on loss, incompletion and diminution. Preferred and
secure spaces, havens for those who find most other places foreign
or even treacherous, close up, disappear, changed into forbidden

ground. Mr Duffy in particular had seemed able to hold his own almost anywhere he found himself, even in Socialist meetings frequented exclusively by working-class agitators. But when both the "eating-house in George's Street where he felt himself safe from the society of Dublin's gilded youth" (Pa 109) and the monastic cell he had created for himself in Chapelizod constrain him, he takes to the streets and into a "public-house at Chapelizod Bridge". The place is as incongruous for Duffy as the "Refreshments Bar" had been for Lenehan, but he makes no concessions to its foreignness:

> The proprietor served him obsequiously but did not venture to talk. There were five or six working-men in the shop discussing the value of a gentleman's estate in County Kildare. They drank at intervals from their huge pint tumblers and smoked, spitting often on the floor and sometimes dragging the sawdust over their spits with their heavy boots. Mr Duffy sat on his stool and gazed at them, without seeing or hearing them. (Pa 116)

He drinks hot punch, Farrington's palliative for humiliation, but for Duffy a cure for the "shock" that attacked his "nerves" (Pa 116).

Establishing his dominance over the terrain by sheer dint of his superior attitude, he orders a second hot punch, but the memory of Mrs Sinico disquiets him here as well: "He began to feel ill at ease" (Pa 116). His ultimate retreat is nearby Phoenix Park, walking "along under the gaunt trees" and "through the bleak alleys where they [he and Emily Sinico] had walked four years before" (Pa 117) – when they discussed terminating their relationship (" in spite of the cold they wandered up and down the roads of the Park for nearly three hours. They agreed to break off their intercourse" – Pa 112). Expulsion from the Garden reverts now to seeking refuge in it, regaining his moral position, but "He felt his moral nature falling into pieces", mocked by the couples in the park engaged in their "venal and furtive loves", "watching him and wished him gone" (Pa 117). Also taunting him is the Serpent, in the reptilian form of "the goods train winding out of Kingsbridge Station, like a worm with a fiery head winding through the darkness, obstinately and laboriously. It passed slowly out of sight; but still he heard in his ears the laborious drone of the engine reiterating the syllables of her name" (Pa 117). E-mi-ly Si-ni-co would now be forever associated with trains and train stations, from Sydney Parade to

Kingsbridge, with expulsion from paradise, with being "outcast from life's feast" (Pa 117). Mrs Sinico had attempted to build a bridge across which she and Mr Duffy could meet, but Duffy had remained obstinate ("We cannot give ourselves . . . we are our own" – Pa 111), and in the end she ignored bridges and took direct access despite the danger, as the railway company representative explained: "The company had always taken every precaution to prevent people from crossing the lines except by the bridges. . . . The deceased had been in the habit of crossing the lines late at night from platform to platform" (Pa 114).

Duffy has been condemned to ultimate loneliness, as Chandler has been reduced to helpless infancy, but as one of their "counterparts" Farrington begins his adventure as solidly irreducible. He is "tall and of great bulk" (Co 86), and one can hardly imagine anyone less likely to "disappear" – or have to fall back totally upon himself (when contemplating the upcoming evening, "he longed to spend it in the bars, drinking with his friends amid the glare of gas and the clatter of glasses" – Co 89). There is a definite completeness about Farrington that seems formidable, a paterfamilias with five children, a pub habitué with many friends, a man of bulk who requires an hour and a half for lunch, according to Mr Alleyne's accusation. That he is so absolutely there is proven, to Mr Shelley's satisfaction: "The chief clerk glanced at the hat-rack but, seeing the row complete, offered no remark" (Co 88). Yet the completeness is deceptive, since Farrington has effected his temporary escape by leaving his hat there as a substitute for himself, his "shepherd's plaid cap" the covering for his "other" self. The copyist at Crosbie and Alleyne is never really there at all, but a bulk that sits in for the man who has his secret life in O'Neill's and Davy Byrne's and the Scotch House and John Mulligan's. Mr Alleyne is coming close to realizing Farrington's non-existence, surveying the Delacour file and discovering that "two letters were missing" (Co 91), while Mr Shelley is also catching on when he asks, "Where were you?" and insists, "I know that game. . . . Five times in one day is a little bit ... " (Co 89). His incomplete sentence echoes Farrington's tendency toward leaving his sentences hanging unfinished, especially during the course of Mr Alleyne's cross-examination ("But Mr Shelley said, sir – " and "I was waiting to see ... " (Co 87, 88), and will become diagnostic in the document Farrington is copying: "He stared intently at the incomplete phrase: *In no case shall the said Bernard Bodley be ...* " (Co 90).

The less Farrington exists at Crosbie and Alleyne's, the more he presumably exists as his real self in the pubs, so that once he gives up on his work and admits to himself that "He couldn't finish it in time" (Co 90), his full attention is given over to the "other" Farrington. He has almost resigned himself to his official non-existence, with his boss's words echoing in his ears: "you'll quit the office instanter! You'll quit this, I'm telling you" (Co 92). The fulfilment of that "real" existence is forecast by his good fortune in obtaining six shillings instead of a mere five for his watch (which he no longer needs since he has failed to function successfully *in time*). It is an expansive Farrington, therefore, who embarks on his revels, feeling himself superior to his "shadow", Higgins (who "never had anything for himself" – Co 92), as well as to Nosey Flynn and Paddy Leonard ("O'Halloran had money but neither of the other two seemed to have any" – Co 94). As in the card game on board Farley's yacht, the non-players fade out to leave the field between the major contestants, Farrington meeting his match at the hands of Weathers as Doyle had at the hands of Routh, so that he becomes progressively aware of his incompleteness: "Funds were running low"; "He cursed his want of money"; "He had done for himself in the office, pawned his watch, spent all his money; and had not even got drunk" (Co 95,97). Arriving home he finds his wife absent, the kitchen empty, the fire gone out and no dinner.

Farrington's son's broken, incomplete phrases, "I'll say a *Hail Mary* ... " (Co 98) – from which *Our Father* is conspicuously absent – ushers in the Maria of "Clay", much as Annie Chandler's "My little man! My little mannie!" (Li 85) had ushered in the great bulk of "the man", Farrington. Whereas Farrington is incomplete without a given name, Maria is incomplete without a surname, and in stature is Farrington's opposite, "a very, very small person indeed" (Cl 99). Diminution as much as depletion characterizes the Maria who leaves the laundry in which she is an important presence ("She was always sent for when the women quarrelled over their tubs and always succeeded in making peace" – Cl 99) to participate in a celebration at the Donnelly household where she is both an honoured guest and an intrusive element. Her presence in the laundry is a result of "the break-up at home" (Cl 100), the original Donnelly household of the brothers who now "were not speaking" to each other (Cl 102). Alphy Donnelly is the piece missing from the Hallowe'en festivities, and "Joe said that Alphy was no brother of his and there was nearly being a row on the head of it" (Cl 104).

The incomplete Maria ("the tip of her nose nearly met the tip of her chin"; in the tram she sits "with her toes barely touching the floor": Cl 101–2) had left behind a gap, a missing piece, as well, when she is toasted with the lifting of a mug of tea by Ginger Mooney, who "was sorry that she hadn't a sup of porter to drink it in" (Cl 101) Maria senses an absence among abundance, knowing that the Donnelly party table would be laden with "plenty of apples and nuts", and decides to supplement it with her special contribution of a "thick slice of plumcake" (Cl 102), but the plumcake never completes its journey to the intended destination.

In its absence ("nowhere could she find it" – Cl 103) the plumcake becomes an "apple of discord", causing animosity among the children sensitive to the accusation of theft, and may have inspired their revenge against Maria with the garden clay as her punishment. She, in turn, is sensitive to her loss, "the failure of her little surprise" and "the two and fourpence she had thrown away for nothing" (Cl 104) – with as disappointing a show for her expenditure as Farrington experienced on his night out. The missing plumcake is only the first of a series of losses, absences, gaps, negations, in a social situation in which Joe denies his brother, "Nobody could find the nutcrackers" (Cl 104), Maria forgets to sing the second verse of her song, and eventually Joe "could not find what he was looking for and in the end he had to ask his wife to tell him where the corkscrew was" (Cl 106).

So much in "Clay" hinges on three relevant gaffes – the loss of the plumcake, the wrong substance on the divination saucer, and the repetition of the first verse of "I Dreamt that I Dwelt" – that a fourth operative factor is too easily glossed over: Joe Donnelly's "smart answer which he had made to the manager" (Cl 104). He may have been as gauche as Farrington, but hardly seems perturbed about any future consequences, and even concedes that the manager "wasn't so bad when you knew how to take him, that he was a decent sort so long as you didn't rub him the wrong way" (Cl 104). Donnelly obviously has that extra element of discretion that his "counterpart" lacks, has a real presence in his work place, and has not irrevocably crossed the line. But his actual smart answer is never recorded, so that any changes he may have made in transmission are lost. Farrington has of course rubbed Mr Alleyne the wrong way, having been overheard "mimicking his North of Ireland accent to amuse Higgins and Miss Parker" (Co 92), and his obsequiousness in the overuse of the word "sir" when dealing with him ever since may have resulted from this first offence. For all his audacity in the insult, he none the less includes the fawning form of address, only to delete it in the pub when capitalizing on his temerity. There is no doubt that Higgins availed himself of the full version in retelling Farrington's tale, and included as well "the way in which Mr Alleyne shook his fist in Farrington's face" (Co 94). That Farrington "had been obliged to offer an abject apology to Mr Alleyne for his impertinence" (Co 92) must also have been excised in Farrington's pub version, although it lingers with him as he leaves the office and remains the sort of burden that he hopes to shake off by getting drunk.

"DEATH BANES AND THE QUICK QUOKE"

From a child's first awareness of the death of an adult (in "The Sisters") to a mature adult's anticipation of the impending death of an ageing relative (in "The Dead"), *Dubliners* enfolds the dying and the dead among the living. Yet, for a long duration during which the focus is on youth and young adults, little attention is given to the determinants of mortality, even though "Eveline" begins the series with a dead sibling and a mother who died insane, Eveline herself subject to heart palpitations. Whereas Father Flynn is acknowledged to have died a disappointed man, there is only the heavy inference that Mrs Hill could not have been anything but a disappointed woman, and certainly Mrs Sinico's case history allies her in this context with Eveline's mother. Gabriel Conroy's morbid thoughts assign Julia Morkan to the realm of the dead, placing him in the role of the concerned spectator at the wake, an extension of the boy visiting the corpse of Father Flynn, who had also been morbidly anticipatory ("I longed to be nearer to it and look upon its deadly work" – Si 9). "The Sisters" is less a story about the boy's *shock* at unexpected death than it is a story of the stages of reactions to expected death, and the fulfilment of those expectations. As an adult Gabriel replays the boy's experience (as if remembering it), and places himself in the uncomfortable position of the safe survivor:

He had caught that haggard look upon her face for a moment when she was singing *Arrayed for the Bridal*. Soon, perhaps, he would be sitting in that same drawing-room, dressed in black, his silk hat on his knees. The blinds would be drawn down and Aunt Kate would be sitting beside him, crying and blowing her nose and telling him how Julia had died. He would cast about in his mind for some words that might console her, and would find only lame and useless ones. Yes, yes: that would happen very soon.   (De 222–3)

Having this evening been presented with the death of his wife's lover, Gabriel cannot quite see himself in the role of a dedicated Michael Furey choosing death to separation from his beloved, but also cannot quite revel in the fact of his being the "safe survivor". He transfers the death from his rival to his foolish aunt, providing himself with a proper part to play as official mourner, aware of his shortcomings, but quite impressively arrayed for the burial.

A composite narrative emerges as the walls of separation that keep discrete the participants in the overall Dublin drama are penetrated: the boy accompanies his aunt to pay his respects to the dead man, but has no language in which to convey those respects and lapses into silence; the man hypothesizes a visit to his dead aunt but he knows that his words of consolation will prove inadequate. A recalcitrant "lover" learns of the death of a woman who had loved him, yet all his words of self-justification fail to rescue him from the solitude of remorse, but years after the death of her lover a woman hears a song that revitalizes the sorrow of her loss. The words of a demented priest are repeated in the presence of a confused child, while the screams of a demented mother resonate in the ears of the daughter who had witnessed her dying. The harbinger of death is heard in the song of an old woman as she sings of marriage, while another old woman sang "in a tiny quavering voice" a song of love and marriage (Cl 106), unaware that her "nephew" has been reduced to tears by his reading of mortality in her haggard face.

There are individual nuances to the ways in which the ghost of her mother haunts Eveline, dividing her between allegiance and fear of duplicating Mrs Hill's death, and the ghost of Michael Furey invoked to haunt Gretta's husband, while she luxuriates in the sad memory, and the ghost of Emily Sinico haunting Duffy more dreadfully in the breach than in the observance. On a communal level the guests at the Morkans' dinner table conjure up an array of musical talent, some still alive but others already departed

("Tietjens, Ilma de Murzka, Campanini, the great Trebelli, Giuglini, Ravelli, Aramburo" – De 199), moving backward in time to arrive at Aunt Kate's choice of someone named Parkinson: "I heard him when he was in his prime and I think he had then the purest tenor voice that was ever put in a man's throat" (De 199). What Kate Morkan succeeds in doing is to remind those assembled of her advanced age, her proximity to death, so that the egregious Mr Browne, not be outdone, is the only one to claim an awareness of Parkinson, but he quickly distances himself from an association with those so old as to be approaching death: "Yes, yes, Miss Morkan is right, said Mr Browne. I remember hearing of old Parkinson but he's too far back for me" (De 200). Parkinson enjoys a unique position in "The Dead", presumably written into the text to be unmemorable to any reader of Joyce's story and consequently a reminder of the transitoriness of reputation and fame. What chances of permanent status then for even so revered a dead hero as Charles Stewart Parnell, who stood out in the rain for hopeless love of his native land and risked death by exposure? "Ivy Day in the Committee Room" marks the moment in time at which Parnell makes the transition from a living ghost to a hollow shade, anticipated in the closure of the preceding story, where Duffy is concerned that a time would come when "he, too, died, ceased to exist, became a memory – if anyone remembered him" (Pa 116). And to further presage the role of Parnell on the eleventh anniversary of his death, Duffy "began to doubt the reality of what memory told him" (Pa 117). The *coup de grâce* to Parnell's potency as a political figure affecting the politics of post-Parnell Ireland is delivered in a succeeding text, when Leopold Bloom muses sadly, "Even Parnell. Ivy day dying out" (Ha 855).

Like Father Flynn, Parnell died a disappointed man whose life, you might say, was crossed, and their presences dominate the tales of death and resurrection that take shape in "The Sisters" and "Ivy Day in the Committee Room". The Parnell story, however, begins with the old caretaker spiritlessly tending the fire in the committee room, an aged relic that returns the image of the paralytic priest of the opening tale:

Old Jack raked the cinders together with a piece of cardboard and spread them judiciously over the whitening dome of coals. When the dome was thinly covered his face lapsed into darkness but, as he set himself to fan the fire again, his crouching shadow ascended the opposite wall and his face slowly re-emerged into light. It was an old man's face, very bony and hairy. The moist blue eyes blinked at the fire and the moist mouth fell open at times, munching once or twice mechanically when it closed.   (Iv 118)

Although still among the living, Old Jack recalls the dead visage of the priest, "very truculent, grey and massive, with black cavernous nostrils and circled by a scanty white fur" (Si 14). The resemblance is not as much a matter of facial features as it is of an ominous inertia that the setting corroborates and incorporates. The cinders in the hearth (ashes to ashes) take on the shape of a death's head, "the whitening dome" that is "thinly covered", while Jack's actual head lapses into darkness. His death is prefigured in the "objective" narration, much as Aunt Julia's is subjectively pre-figured in her nephew's musings, and the spirit that leaves his inert body is a "crouching shadow" that ascends the wall on the other side (with Father Flynn "You couldn't tell when the breath went out of him" – Si 15). The only two full dates in *Dubliners* are the death dates of Flynn and Parnell: "July 1st, 1895" (Si 12) and "*6th October 1891*" (Iv 134). And an intimation of a return to life is tentatively offered when Jack's face is seen re-emerging into the light.

Those who gather in the room in desultory fashion are placing themselves in a position to receive the resurrected Parnell on this day that might well augur his potential return. The welcoming committee at first consists of only Jack and Mat O'Connor, so that each arrival is at least momentarily an avatar of the fallen Chief, yet O'Connor himself, the most sympathetic character in the story, already possesses a Parnellian characteristic: he had been out in the rain canvassing for votes and now has taken refuge back in ward headquarters because "his boots let in the wet" (Iv 119): Parnell had been out on the campaign trail and his feet got wet in the rain in Brighton, resulting in the pneumonia that brought on his death, but he of course continued on in the wet despite the danger. Removed from the significance of Parnell's legacy the canvassers hardly know just what it is that they are waiting for, Tierney's payment or his gift of bottles of stout, or even the candidate himself. As the "candidate", Tierney is distinctly unlike his predecessor, but none the less claims in part to have inherited his mantle, even though he is presented to potential voters by his agent Henchy as someone who *"doesn't belong to any party, good, bad or indifferent"* (Iv 131).

The "candidates" for the role of the returned Parnell troop in, Hynes and Henchy and Father Keon and Lyons and Crofton, and even the pub boy; most of them to stay on, unsure what they are waiting for but inauspiciously constituting themselves as a potential reception committee for the Shade. Joe Hynes even arrives twice, his second coming more politely received by Henchy than his first, but the boy from the Black Eagle pub also has a second coming, the return visit with the borrowed corkscrew. Father Keon in particular calls attention to himself as a dead man pretending to be alive ("a poor actor"), risen from the grave, with a recognizable death's head: "His face, shining with raindrops, had the appearance of damp yellow cheese save where two rosy spots indicated the cheekbones. He opened his very long mouth suddenly to express disappointment" (Iv 125) – another disappointed man of the cloth, moribund and yellowing.

"Ivy Day" shares with all of the *Dubliners* stories the plethora of gnomonic implications of absences and deletions, but most of them in this instance band together to retell elliptically facets of the Parnell story. Any expectation of a possible successor to Parnell brings forward only an inheritor to the betrayal of Parnell and other nationalist leaders in Irish history, someone like "a certain nobleman with a cock-eye . . . that'd sell his country for fourpence" – in other words, "a lineal descendant of Major Sirr" (Iv 125). Quite expectedly Joe Hynes' commemorative verse assigns betrayal as the cause of the Chief's death in analogy with that of the Saviour:

> . . . *treachery*
> *Sundered him from the thing he loved.*
> *Shame on the coward caitiff hands*
> *That smote their Lord or with a kiss*
> *Betrayed him to the rabble-rout*
> *Of fawning priests . . .* (Iv 134)

The conventional forms carried over by versifier Hynes also offer the configuration of resurrection in terms of fire, *"his spirit may / Rise, like the Phoenix from the flames"* (Iv 135), all the more potent when linked with the image of Parnell's symbolic cremation: *"Erin's hopes and Erin's dreams / Perish upon her monarch's pyre"* (Iv 134). The inadequate glow from the cinder-laden fireplace, therefore, places the hopes of a returned Parnell in that hearth in which the annoyed Henchy "spat so copiously that he nearly put out the fire which uttered a hissing protest" (Iv 124). Hynes, of course, carries the Parnell banner into the hostile region of the committee room, but Henchy denies him even a *"spark* of manhood" and Old Jack refuses Hynes a *"warm* welcome" (Iv 124; emphasis added). Loyal Joe Hynes signals his allegiance when he turns back his collar and displays "an ivy leaf in the lapel" (Iv 122), duplicating the earlier gesture of the loyal Mat O'Connor at the fireplace: "the flame lit up a leaf of dark glossy ivy in the lapel of his coat" (Iv 119). The "presence" of Parnell in Tierney's cave is solely in the symbolic piece of ivy – that is, like the fire, dying out.

Hynes carries the cudgels for all that remains of Charles Stewart Parnell and has no compunction in identifying "Tricky Dicky Tierney" as the betrayer: " – If this man was alive, he said, pointing to the leaf, we'd have no talk of an address of welcome", referring to Tierney's concession to the anticipated visit of King Edward VII. Old Jack, who claims to offer no "warm welcome" to Hynes, chimes in with his brand of nostalgia (" – Musha, God be with them times! said the old man. There was some life in it then" – Iv 122). Tierney's potential for betrayal is acknowledged even by Henchy, who appropriates the "Tricky Dicky" appellation from the Hynes he mistrusts and sneeringly repeats the candidate's promise of *"I won't forget you, you may be sure"*, condemning him to a soulless existence ("Blast his soul!"), and exposing Tierney's mean origins, where Tierney "first saw the light" (Iv 123). Tierney's claim – should he ever be willing to make it – as Parnell's inheritor is consequently denied even by his own "agent", but in the process of discussing the address of welcome to the British King (which Henchy does champion, irrevocably linking him with Tierney), the ironic replacement for Parnell materializes.

Against the incredulity of Bantam Lyons and Mat O'Connor, Henchy advances the parallel between Ireland's Uncrowned King and Britain's monarch, who had long remained uncrowned because of Victoria's longevity, "till the man was grey". Actually the "parallel" becomes four-sided: Parnell is cited in his opposition to the British throne ("Why should we welcome the King of England? Didn't Parnell himself ..."), but O'Connor is prevented from completing his sentence, as is Lyons, who says, regarding Edward's immorality: "King Edward's life, you know, is not the very ..." (Iv 132). Parnell's parallel "immorality" identifies him now with

Edward, so that Lyons undercuts Parnell's legitimacy by asserting, "Do you think now after what he did Parnell was a fit man to lead us? And why, then, would we do it for Edward the Seventh?" (Iv 132). What differentiates Parnell from the reigning King of England is merely the fact that one is dead and the other alive ("Parnell, said Mr Henchy, is dead"), so that even the loyalist O'Connor succeeds in "burying" Parnell: "We all respect him now that he's dead and gone" (Iv 132). (The King is dead, long live the King!) In an ironic exchange, Edward Rex steps into Parnell's shoes at this existential moment in, of all places, Dublin's "ROYAL EXCHANGE WARD" (Iv 119). Everything else that would impede the "takeover" fades away as a certain nothingness takes possession: there are no tumblers to drink from, but O'Connor is willing to drink from the bottle ("it's better than nothing" – Iv 129); no corkscrew with which to open the bottles, but one is borrowed temporarily, only to be prematurely returned so as not to be there to accommodate the new arrivals; Crofton distinguishes himself by having "nothing to say"; the Conservatives have "withdrawn their man"; Tierney "doesn't belong to any party"; "the factories down by the quays" are "idle" (Iv 131). Only Edward VII fills the vacuum, although Henchy may object when he asks, "where's the analogy between the two cases?" (Iv 132).

Parnell's fall from grace (as well as from power) is later reduced by analogy when Mr Kernan falls down the pub lavatory steps in "Grace", and the attempts to resurrect him are initiated by Mr Power (a fragment from Hynes's epitaph for Parnell might serve as an epitaph for Kernan's tale: *"raised to glory from the mire"* – Iv 134). Kernan's drop into the lower depths is hardly fatal, but for a while he is "quite helpless", lying "curled up" in a foetal position, and unresponsive to the attempts made to "lift him up" (Gr 150). The prostrate form is encircled by the other pub customers ("In two minutes he was surrounded by a ring of men" – Gr 150), and there is a relentlessness about that tight encirclement that only Power can eventually manage to break: "The ring of onlookers distended and closed again elastically"; "He looked at the circle of faces and then, understanding, strove to rise to his feet" (Gr 151). The "dead" Kernan has had his glimpse of the underworld and wrenches himself back to life, constantly attempting to deny his death: " 's nothing", he repeats over and over again (Gr 151,152,153).

The vocabulary of negation serves as the dominant linguistic field of play in "Grace", and so persistent is every character in speaking in the negative, even to the extent of phrasing the positive in double negatives, that the narrational process incorporates the attitudes of the people involved. Kernan was blessed with two benefactors, the unknown young man in the cycling suit who is the first rescuer, and then Power who saves Kernan from arrest (as Corny Kelleher will for the prostrate Stephen Dedalus in *Ulysses*): the cyclist responds to Kernan's gratitude with a casual "Not at all" (Gr 152), so that when Mrs Kernan expresses her gratitude to Power for bringing her husband home, the echoed response is also "Not at all" (Gr 155). The *King Lear* equation of "Nothing will come of nothing" surfaces in this exchange between Kernan's wife and Jack Power, when she asks about Kernan's drinking companions:

> Mr Power shook his head but said nothing.
> – I'm so sorry, she continued, that I've nothing in the house to offer you.   (Gr 155)

Kernan in recuperation is still eager to make light of the incident, to reduce it to non-existence, and savours the word of negation in a comic exchange with his wife when he has so obviously been overlooked as the bottles of stout are being served: "Have you nothing for me, duckie?" – and to his wife's caustic reply he persists with "Nothing for poor little hubby!" (Gr 162).

Each of the participants in the comedy has an opportunity to speak in the negative, especially the "comforters" intent on surrounding Kernan and leading him to the retreat at the Gardiner Street church. Power initiated the process even before his conversation with Mrs Kernan: back in the pub he deflected his friend's attempt to stand a drink to the stranger in the cycling suit with a curt "Not now. Not now" (Gr 152). He reminds Kernan that had he been arrested it would have meant jail "without the option of a fine" (Gr 160); he stresses the importance of getting to the church on time by insisting that "we musn't be late" (Gr 162); he assures Kernan that Father Purdon "won't be too hard on us" (Gr 164); he is certain that "Dowling was no German" (Gr 169) and that "None of the Grays was any good" (Gr 170); and as the Cunningham plan to resurrect the fallen Kernan seems just about set, "Mr Power said nothing. He felt completely outgeneralled" (Gr 171). Whereas Power may feel backed into a negative corner from the beginning of his dealings with Tom Kernan, Martin Cunningham starts out in a basically positive mode, unaffected by the nay-sayings and negatives, but as soon as he needs to dissemble, to mask the ulterior intentions of the trio of comforters, he lapses into the eliding negation: when Kernan wants to know "What's in the wind?" Cunningham's response is "O, it's nothing" (Gr 162). Thereafter he too follows along the same line, so that Father Purdon's sermon is "not exactly a sermon" (Gr 165), Father Tom Burke "didn't preach what was quite orthodox" (Gr 165), and concerning the Popes of Rome, "Not one of them, not the biggest drunkard, not the most ... out-and-out ruffian, not one of them ever preached *ex cathedra* a word of false doctrine" (Gr 168). And Cunningham even gives voice to the negative outcry of those who opposed the doctrine of papal infallibility: "No! They wouldn't have it!" (Gr 169). His final word, however, once Kernan has been strategically encircled but weakly offers his last protest regarding the necessity of a candle, is a quite confident "O yes" (Gr 171).

The "least" of the three conspirators is M'Coy, whose presence in the august company of Power and Cunningham goes unexplained, especially since Jack Power resents M'Coy's use of his given name and "could not forget" the dishonest ploy of borrowing valises (a ploy that Leopold Bloom will carefully circumvent when he meets M'Coy in *Ulysses*) "to fulfil imaginary engagements" (Gr 160). Other than the presumed necessity for a *trio* of comforters is the possibility that M'Coy's new job as "secretary to the City Coroner" qualifies him in this venture, just as Bloom's experience in the insurance business qualifies him to accompany Cunningham and Power to visit Dignam's widow. That M'Coy's "new office made him professionally interested in Mr Kernan's case" (Gr 158) might well be intended to bring an awareness to Kernan of his brush with death. M'Coy's opening remark, solicitous as it is, is phrased in the negative, "It doesn't pain you now?" (Gr 158), and thereafter he merely follows the line of least resistance, dissembling in his own way, as when he "pretended he had never heard the story" of "65, catch your cabbage" (Gr 161). He echoes Kernan's disdain for the police ("It's better to have nothing to say to them" – Gr 161), but echoes Cunningham's respect for the Jesuits: "There's no mistake about it, said M'Coy, if you want a thing well done and no flies about it" (Gr 163). All of his negatives consistently serve to second the statements made by the others, all and any of the others, so that whatever purpose was intended in including M'Coy, he is a secondary line of defence, despite his gaucheries. Fogarty's arrival, however, was unplanned for, and it is apparent that he is unaware of the need to play everything in the double negative: he rushes in to contradict Cunningham with an uncompromising "No, no. . . . I think you're wrong there" (Gr 167), inadvertently echoed when Cunningham quotes the dissenters on papal infallibility, and finally when Kernan musters his courage in his own dissembling dissent: "No, damn it all, I bar the candles!" (Gr 171).

At the back of the scheme worked out by the conspirators/ comforters is the necessity to "beat the devil", to save Kernan from damnation by disguises that the devil will not recognize. Power may be subliminally reacting to direct naming as detrimental to their scheme when "he did not relish the use of his Christian name" (Gr 160) by M'Coy (whose Christian name never appears in *Dubliners*), and Cunningham may be elliptically cunning when he is willing to admit that "we're a nice collection of scoundrels, one and all" (Gr 163) – "scoundrels" slotted in to serve in lieu of "sinners". While on one hand they are intent on saving Kernan from backsliding ("he had not been in the pale of the Church for twenty years" – Gr 157) by encircling him within the confines of the Church, on the other hand they are attending Kernan's wake and fooling the devil by pretending that Kernan is still alive. Kernan as a revivified corpse is "propped up in the bed by pillows and the little colour in his puffy cheeks made them resemble warm cinders" (Gr 156). Cunningham's demeanour projects his funereal pose as he speaks "gravely", only to have Kernan reply "equally gravely" (Gr 160), while the intrusive Fogarty, who brings whisky to the wake, is even capable of a gravity that is beyond words as he "drank gravely" (Gr 168). (The use of this adverbial indicator is expanded when the Cunninghams and Powers and Dedaluses and Blooms assemble at Prospect Cemetery in Glasnevin for Dignam's funeral. Kernan's house is "on the Glasnevin road" and Fogarty is a nearby neighbour with a "small shop on Glasnevin Road" – (Gr 154, 166.)

Beating the devil by confusing him as to who is who becomes a game of musical chairs in "Grace", where characters mysteriously appear out of nowhere and others disappear or remain nameless. The first mystery is in identifying the unconscious Kernan, and once Power does just that he questions Kernan about his drinking companions, who had quickly dispersed. Kernan himself remains vague about one of the two ("I don't know his name. Damn it now, what's his name? Little chap with sandy hair ... " – Gr 159), but identifies Harford as the other, only to have Harford, whose "fellow-travellers had never consented to overlook his origin" (Gr 159), turn up at the Gardiner Street church. The Good Samaritan appears and disappears, first refusing to be thanked ("Don't mention it") and then declining a repeated offer of a drink with a succinct "Another time" (Gr 153). When the three plotters assemble, Mrs Kernan gives them chairs by the fire and quickly bows out, returning with a tray of glasses and bottles, but when Power offers "her his chair", she declines and leaves again (Gr 161). Later, she reappears to usher the unexpected Mr Fogarty into the bedroom – again absenting herself – and "he sat down with the company on equal terms" (Gr 166). Yet there is no indication where he managed to locate a chair for himself, but is described as "sitting on a small area of the chair" (Gr 167). Had Power offered Mrs Kernan his chair because there was no other? Is Fogarty now sitting in Power's chair which Power again abandoned to serve the whisky? The question of enough seating is not irrelevant considering the plans for the visit to the retreat.

That the "transept of the Jesuit Church in Gardiner Street was almost full" (Gr 172) is understandable considering that Power had already expected that "it is sure to be crammed to the doors" (Gr 162), necessitating an early arrival for the group. The final segment of "Grace", therefore, presents them already seated, with no explanation as to how they had succeeded in seating themselves:

> In one of the benches near the pulpit sat Mr Cunningham and Mr Kernan. In the bench behind sat Mr M'Coy alone: and in the bench behind him sat Mr Power and Mr Fogarty. Mr M'Coy had tried unsuccessfully to find a place in the bench with the others and, when the party had settled in the form of a quincunx, he had tried unsuccessfully to make comic remarks. As these had not been well received he had desisted.   (Gr 172)

Unless they arrived to find most of the seats already occupied and took the five available, easing M'Coy out of either set of two seats that were available together, there may have been alterations in their announced plans, which were that the three plotters were to meet at "Half-seven at M'Auley's" (Gr 162) – a plan into which Kernan was to be accommodated. Fogarty is again the unexpected guest, but now apparently included. To meet at a pub, however, may not have been the best idea, considering Kernan's predilection for boose (his tipple was rum on the night of his fall, but will be gin by the time he returns in *Ulysses*). Also, changes may have been made to ascertain that Kernan would not "funk it", and Cunningham could have arranged to collect Kernan, while Power and Fogarty may have met somewhere, and M'Coy eased out of the arrangements. Whether they arrived in the groupings suggested by their seating, or came together as a group, they are now dispersed and divided, and the M'Coy who had once been in the inner circle now the odd-man-out.

Humpty-Dumpty Kernan has had a great fall, and the King's men of Dublin Castle are attempting to put him together again, but Tom Kernan may have his own plans for his resurrection that do not include either his friends or his wife or the Roman Catholic Church ("his line of life had not been the shortest distance between two points" – Gr 158). His religious totem is his silk hat, as we have seen earlier in another context, and on the basis of agreeing to go to the retreat his damaged hat "had been rehabilitated by his wife" (Gr 173), and he is very careful with it in the church. Kernan's God may not be identical with that of Father Purdon, but someone whom he venerates and with whom he identifies:

> Mr Kernan was a commercial traveller of the old school which believed in the dignity of its calling. He had never been seen in the city without a silk hat of some decency and a pair of gaiters. By grace of these two articles of clothing, he said, a man could always pass muster. He carried on the tradition of his Napoleon, the great Blackwhite, whose memory he evoked at times by legend and mimicry. (Gr 153–4)

The mixture of the Church (*calling, grace*) and the military (*Napoleon, muster*) creates its own *legend*, and Kernan in his *gaiters* considers himself episcopal in his *dignity*.

Whatever has happened to the great Blackwhite, his funeral must have been an auspicious occasion that Kernan might want for himself, one like the funeral described by another commercial traveller, Willy Loman, for his venerated predecessor:

> His name was Dave Singleman. And he was eighty-four-years old, and drummed merchandise in thirty-one states. . . . when he died – and by the way he died the death of a salesman . . . hundreds of salesmen and buyers were at his funeral. . . . In those

days there was personality in it. . . . There was respect and gratitude in it. Today, it's all cut and dried.

The gap between Blackwhite and Kernan complements the gap between Singleman and Loman, Kernan's vocation no longer one of respect and gratitude: "Modern business methods had spared him only so far as to allow him a little office in Crowe Street" (Gr 154).

In "Hades" the new Kernan ("We'll make a new man of him", Power had promised Mrs Kernan – Gr 155) appears at the paltry funeral of the insignificant Paddy Dignam, one of a dozen mourners (plus the intrusive "M'Intosh"), commenting that "the cemetery is a treacherous place", so that he protects himself by putting his hat back on (Ha 656–8). He expresses his critical attitude toward the priest reading the service over Dignam, flaunting his backsliding to fellow-convert Bloom by praising the ceremony at the Protestant cemetery: "The service of the Irish church used in Mount Jerome is simpler, more impressive I might say" (Ha 665–6). In voicing the essence of that service Kernan may be pointing to his own "line of life" after the attempts by his friends to renew him along their own lines: "*I am the resurrection and the life*. That touches a man's inmost heart" (Ha 670). Whatever changes may have taken place in his relationship to his solicitous friends remains vague, except that Kernan is not in the carriage with Cunningham and Power, who do comment obliquely about him when the carriage passes within the Kernan–Fogarty neighbourhood (Glasnevin Road):

– I wonder how is our friend Fogarty getting on, Mr Power said.
– Better ask Tom Kernan, Mr Dedalus said.
– How is that? Martin Cunningham said. Left him weeping, I suppose?
– Though lost to sight, Mr Dedalus said, to memory dear.

(Ha 454–7)

Fogarty may have proved to be the most vulnerable of the lot for Kernan's revenge on his "benefactors", especially since he is the neighbourhood grocer with a precarious business, and Kernan was "aware that there was a small account for groceries unsettled between him and Mr Fogarty" (Gr 166). Kernan could have settled his accounts with Fogarty by keeping the outstanding account unsettled, and would have had ulterior motives regarding the bringer of the whisky he himself was not allowed to drink. With his tongue painful and causing his slurred speech, Kernan could not have helped noticing Fogarty's "neat enunciation", or that as someone whose "state of grace" was the object of so much directed attention Kernan again was disadvantaged by the presence of a grocer who "bore himself with a certain grace" (Gr 166).

"TO IDENDIFINE THE INDIVIDUONE"

The physical law that two bodies cannot occupy the same space governs much of the social dynamics of *Dubliners*, in a society of depleted possibilities and diminished opportunities, with the game of "musical chairs" operative in parts of "Ivy Day" and "Grace", and even more "musical" motifs operative in "A Mother" and "The Dead". Yet, without losing the sharp sense of individual loss, these tales of public life also indicate areas in which multiple bodies *do* manage to occupy the same space – in group identity. The clusters in the Gardiner Street church are of the Kernan-rehabilitation contingent and the pocket of businessmen that includes Harford (Kernan's erstwhile friend), mayor-maker Fanning, Michael Grimes, Dan Hogan's nephew and "poor O'Carroll", another old Kernan friend, very much in decline – these isolated from the extensive crowd by their group identities. In the political committee room the individuals are identifiable in their relationship to either Parnell or to Tierney, shifting the ground as they are affected by external influences (including bottles of stout), but they are also rearranged once a third factor, King Edward, enters the equation. By contrast, the much larger collection of guests in "The Dead" results in various named and unnamed supernumeraries, until the focus eventually shifts away from the concern of the Morkans for their guests, and Gabriel's overwhelming accumulation of concerns in regard to Lily, Miss Ivors, his auditors, and finally to his wife, so that once the general category of dinner-party participants disintegrates, the threesome of Gabriel, Gretta and Michael Furey (who had no function as a guest of the Morkans) establishes its supremacy.

In "A Mother" the cast of characters appears to be definite and distinct (Hoppy Holohan, Mrs Kearney and Kathleen Kearney – with Mr Kearney in the wings) until the group rearranges itself backstage at the Antient Concert Rooms. The gravitational movement should logically be *toward the stage* on which Kathleen and the other *artistes* will perform, assuming that it is musical performance that will be the result of the combined efforts of Mrs Kearney and Holohan, but the centrifugal force of the underlying situation propels them instead into two opposing backstage camps:

> In one corner were Mr Holohan, Mr Fitzpatrick, Miss Beirne, two of the stewards, the baritone, the bass, and Mr O'Madden Burke. . . . In another corner of the room were Mrs Kearney and her husband, Mr Bell, Miss Healy, and the young lady who had recited the patriotic piece. (Mo 147–8)

The sides are disproportionate to begin with, overbalanced in favour of that vague but powerful group, the Committee, so that a handful of unorganized individuals appear to stand out against a collective force. But even within the meagre ranks one potential defector exists in Miss Healy, who "wanted to join the other group but did not like to do so because she was a great friend of Kathleen's and the Kearneys had often invited her to their house" (Mo 148). When the battle is actually engaged, Miss Healy is the relevant defector when it is learned that she had "kindly consented to play one or two accompaniments", replacing Kathleen (Mo 149). It eventually becomes apparent that only one combatant is engaged in battle with the Committee and its combined allies, Mrs Kearney.

Mrs Kearney's weakness is her inability to recognize collective opposition ("I haven't seen any Committee, said Mrs Kearney angrily" – Mo 148), but this may be explained in terms of group dynamics in that a committee is an entity that hides behind itself. Mrs Kearney has indeed seen a Committee but failed to recognize either its combined strength or its capacity for splintering whenever that method proves convenient. Somewhere behind or within or synonymous with the *Eire Abu* Society is this Committee, and although he deflects responsibility away from himself by deferring to the "faceless" Committee, Holohan logically belongs to it. More formidable, of course, is Mr Fitzpatrick, who certainly can speak and act for the group, but he too prefers to remain evasive, calling upon the larger entity that Mrs Kearney cannot get at. Even Miss Beirne "stands in" for the Committee, but her veil of insignificance is very effective camouflage:

> Mrs Kearney . . . went all over the building looking for Mr
> Holohan or Mr Fitzpatrick. She could find neither. She asked one
> of the stewards was any member of the Committee in the hall
> and, after a great deal of trouble, a steward brought out a little
> woman named Miss Beirne to whom Mrs Kearney explained that
> she wanted to see one of the secretaries. Miss Beirne expected
> them any minute and asked could she do anything. Mrs Kearney
> looked searchingly at the oldish face which was screwed into an
> expression of trustfulness and enthusiasm and answered:
> – No, thank you!   (Mo 141–2)

Miss Beirne's mask succeeds in putting her off, primarily because
even as a woman Mrs Kearney does not accept the possibility of
any authority vested in a woman, yet she is exact in her observation
that Kathleen is being victimized because "They thought they had
only a girl to deal with and that, therefore, they could ride rough-
shod over her. But she would show them their mistake. They
wouldn't have dared to have treated her like that if she had been a
man" (Mo 148). She attempts to bypass the woman and get to
masculine authority, but Mr Kearney will prove to be an ineffectual
component in his wife's battle plans and will put into question the
monolith of masculine authority, while Miss Beirne's self-effacing
demeanour should have been recognized as a front for the
composite Committee. Masculine authority in "A Mother" is
exemplied by the deceptive "Mr Holohan in his limping and
devious courses" (Mo 144).

From the beginning Mrs Kearney assumed that she had usurped
an important measure of authority from the bumbling Holohan:
"As Mr Holohan was a novice in such delicate matters as the
wording of bills and the disposing of items for a programme Mrs
Kearney helped him. She had tact. She knew what *artistes* should
go into capitals and what *artistes* should go into small type" (Mo
138). (Holohan is a "novice" only in the eyes of someone who
exults in having been "educated in a high-class convent" – Mo 136.)
Yet when the first concert is about to begin, her tactful ministra-
tions are nowhere apparent, since she has obviously been circum-
vented without being consulted: "Mr Holohan admitted that the
artistes were no good but the Committee, he said, had decided to let
the first three concerts go as they pleased and reserve all the talent
for Saturday night. Mrs Kearney said nothing but, as the mediocre
items followed one another on the platform . . . " (Mo 140). The

Committee's next surprise is to cancel the Friday concert and concentrate on Saturday's, a plan that proves to be quite successful, so that it is at the point at which the Committee's manoeuvrings vindicate them that Mrs Kearney becomes intransigent and withdraws Kathleen from the limelight. There is no question that she has been shortchanged, but she has also been outflanked by an opponent who correctly gauged her deviousness: Mrs Kearney was secretly intent on winning a battle that she had long since lost, a battle that cannot now be won.

At the root of the disaster is Mrs Kearney's complex problem of identity, both as self and as gender-identified: she is as ambivalent about being Mrs Kearney as she is of Kathleen being Miss Kearney, and uncertain as to how to negotiate the difference between being a woman and being the "lady" that a woman is expected to be. Her ivory manners protect her only as long as she does not exceed the limits of propriety, so at first she checks her inclination to insult Mr Fitzpatrick by mimicry ("she knew that it would not be ladylike to do that" – Mo 141), but Fitzpatrick's vacuousness (his "white vacant face", his "vacant smile" – Mo 139, 140) finally goads her into stepping across the line and offending more than just the Committee: "I thought you were a lady", snorts Hoppy Holohan, turning it also into an insult: "That's a nice lady! . . . O, she's a nice lady" (Mo 149). Although she has no intention of complying with society's dictates regarding "ladylike" behaviour, she does realize that she must present the necessary façade (the vacant ladylike face), but her inner self rebels against the delimiting propriety.

It is actually as Miss Devlin that this "mother" performs, never having reconciled herself to the inevitable, that the Ormond Quay bootmaker "would wear better than a romantic person" (in reality "she never put her own romantic ideas away" – Mo 137). She remains Miss Devlin and replicates herself in Kathleen as a supplementary Miss Devlin (mother was "educated in a high-class convent where she had learned French and music" – Mo 136; daughter was sent to "a good convent, where she learned French and music" – Mo 137). Whereas the overt scheme was that Kathleen would succeed where her mother had not, the covert scheme was that Kathleen would fail just as her mother had failed, proving that it is the "Committee" that was to blame. (Mr Kearney may have his own scheme, perhaps aware that Miss Devlin had felt obligated to marry the unromantic person because "she drew near the limit and her friends began to loosen their tongues about her", so that by "paying a small sum every week into a society he ensured for both his daughters a dowry of one hundred pounds each when they came to the age of twenty-four" – Mo 137.) The group of supporters that had gathered around the ladylike Mrs Kearney disintegrates, and in the final stages she loses the support of her husband and daughter as well: "She stood at the door, haggard with rage, arguing with her husband and daughter, gesticulating with them" (Mo 149). In the end, these are the only ones she can dominate, sending her husband out for a cab and taking physical possession of Kathleen ("Mrs Kearney wrapped the cloak round her daughter" – Mo 149), and it is an an unrelenting Miss Devlin that she stalks out.

The anonymous members of the audience in the Antient Concert Rooms provide the first significant body of outsiders in the tight web of Dubliners who comprise the *dramatis personae* of the volume. They are not, however, aware of the real drama being played out backstage, but have come to be entertained by the *artistes*, and their insignificance as "participating" Dubliners is particularly apparent on the second night when "the house was filled with paper" (Mo 140) – non-paying spectators, implying their remoteness from the focal point of involvement. How different, then, the indeterminate number of "others" in "The Dead", where only a small handful dominate stage centre but are absorbed into a larger social framework of auditors and viewers. It is significant that when the social occasion is first alluded to it is as "the Misses Morkan's annual dance" (De 175), and many more of the guests are among those dancing than actually appear at the dinner-table in the centre of the events, reserved apparently for a certain "inner circle". (The table being prepared suggests that it is too small for everyone at the party: "Two square tables placed end to end" – De 182.) Among the various guests there exists an exterior world of supernumeraries, such as those who drifted away when Mary Jane was playing her Academy piece but reassembled in the doorway to applaud once it was over, and later when the Three Graces have been toasted, the "acclamation which followed was taken up beyond the door of the supper-room by many of the other guests" (De 205). Even more "external" is a crowd that only exists in speculation: "People, perhaps, were standing in the snow on the quay outside, gazing up at the lighted windows and listening to the waltz music" (De 202).

The stories of public life contribute to an awareness of the world outside, without losing sight of the individual dramas being intimately enacted in small pockets of interrelated people. But the possibility surfaces that those who assume that they are the actors are in other configurations mere spectators, that their claims to individuality are somehow overextended. The grouping around the two square tables placed end to end and covered with a cloth consists of family, close friends and those who are being "courted", a promising new tenor (Bartell D'Arcy) and Mary Jane's affluent pupils. The named diners are Gabriel and Gretta, Aunts Kate and Julia, niece Mary Jane, Freddy Malins and his mother, D'Arcy and Browne, Miss Furlong, Miss Daly and Miss Higgins – an even dozen, if the last three are the students on whom Mary Jane waited "and saw that they got the best slices" (De 197). Molly Ivors had been expected to dine with them, and would have been the thirteenth at table, so that once again there is the sense of a game of musical chairs, of fewer places available than people to occupy them, of individuals standing in for each other or, conversely, playing more parts than merely their own. From the very opening Lily is "run off her feet" because she is expected to be in two places at once: "Hardly had she brought one gentleman into the little pantry behind the office on the ground floor and helped him off with his overcoat than the wheezy hall-door bell clanged again and she had to scamper along the bare hallway to let in another guest" (De 175). This is the same Lily who later in the evening "went from guest to guest with a dish of hot floury potatoes" (De 197), three of which she holds back to serve to Gabriel when he is ready to fill his plate – the ubiquitous servant.

Lily's capacity to be in two places at once is paralleled by her dual personality, the split between the Lily who *was* and the Lily who *is*. Gabriel has difficulty in "identifying" her, and in his configuration she is still the schoolgirl that evolved from the child he remembers ("Gabriel had known her when she was a child and used to sit on the lowest step nursing a rag doll" – De 177), but when corrected regarding her present status, he blunders once again. His version of the new Lily is that of a prospective bride, but Lily's "bitter and sudden retort" (De 179) suggests quite a different young woman, which also makes her a different person from the one that her employers are familiar with. Whereas the "fixed" description of her insists that "Lily seldom made a mistake in the orders so that she got on well with her three mistresses. They were fussy, that was all. But the only thing they would not stand was back answers" (De 176), the contemporary Lily of the bitter-and-sudden-retort is not just a momentary aberration, and Kate Morkan acknowledges that "She's not the girl she was at all" (De 181). That Gabriel still assumes that she is at school suggests how infrequently he visits his aunts on Usher's Island, and it is quite possible that he has not been there since last year's party.

As a social unit the assembled guests at the soirée (assuming that "Everybody who knew them came to it" – De 175) are an odd assortment, combining the familial with some rather inexplicable inclusions. Bartell D'Arcy is obviously a first-timer (unfamiliar with the routine, he has to be convinced to allow his glass to be filled for the toast), and if he has been allowed in so that he could sing for his supper, he is certainly a disappointment. On the other hand, Browne is a regular, although there are indications that he is not particularly appreciated, someone about whom the hostesses can complain. It is not easy to accept the notion that the Morkans find it necessary to include a token Protestant, but it is apparent that they use Browne as something of a scapegoat, complaining that "He has been laid on here like the gas" (De 206), even blaming him for Freddy Malins's drunkenness, an absurdity since Freddy arrived already drunk. The yearly ritual of worrying whether Freddy "might turn up screwed" (De 176) makes him a worrisome guest to accept, but presumably it is his mother's yearly visit from Glasgow that accounts for the invitation extending to her son as well.

Ritual also involves Gabriel's role as Freddy's keeper, and in an odd way the two men are linked in the minds of the two Miss Morkans: "Freddy Malins always came late but they wondered what could be keeping Gabriel" (De 176). Gabriel's "significance" to his aunts at this juncture is strictly in terms of taking care of Freddy, so that when they realize that Gretta has arrived they "asked was Gabriel with her" (De 177), hardly a logical question. To associate Gabriel Conroy with Freddy Malins, much less to actually conflate the two, seems ludicrous, yet the two are coincidentally linked, especially as their arrivals are almost simultaneous: "It's only Freddy, Kate, and Gabriel with him", explains Aunt Julia, and Freddy is discovered to be "of Gabriel's size and build" (De 184). As Freddy's guardian Gabriel is quick to fulfil his obligation and extricate himself as quickly as possible, and his aunt suddenly becomes complicit in abandoning Freddy and claiming Gabriel ("But come on, Gabriel, into the drawing-room" – De 185).

As his aunt's favourite and something of a guest of honour Gabriel is awkward and out of place at this annual event, and spends much of the evening not only yearning to be outside but often on the move in the various rooms of the house, at first "discomposed" by Lily's retort (De 179) and later inexplicably restless. His movements can be choreographed even before he is drawn into the "lancers": somehow he has managed to elude his aunt and remove himself from the drawing-room, only to find himself "discomposed" in the music room by Mary Jane's playing (that it "had no melody for him" is belied when we learn that "she was playing again the opening *melody*" – De 186,187, emphasis added). Politeness traps him into staying in this room, although he is also irritated her by a photograph of his mother, reminding him of her attitude toward Gretta: "Some slighting phrases she had used still rankled in his memory" (De 187). Politeness also probably dictated his participation in the lancers, where he "found himself partnered with Miss Ivors" (De 187). It is ironic that Aunt Kate complains that "we're so short of ladies to-night" (De 184), considering Gabriel's continued discomposition in his contact with various females, and he is sufficiently disconcerted by Molly Ivors to lose control of his own movements, so that she has to guide him in the dance: "Come, we cross now" (De 188). "When the lancers were over Gabriel went away to a remote corner of the room where Freddy Malins' mother was sitting" (De 190), surely an indication that he is desperate for a safe harbour, for his own *querencia*, but Gretta tracks him to his lair and berates him for both his treatment of Molly and refusal to take her on holiday to the Aran Isles. Her summation of him ("There's a nice husband for you, Mrs Malins" – De 191) provides one of many labels that serve to pin Gabriel Conroy down, to identify him, although the entire process succeeds instead in splitting him into varying identities.

The game of musical chairs, supplemented with the missteps in the dance, continues when Gabriel eludes the two women soon after: "When he saw Freddy Malins coming across the room to visit his mother Gabriel left the chair free for him and retired into the embrasure of the window" (De 191). Essentially locked into his own thoughts of his after-dinner speech, he is again routed out by Aunt Julia singing, yet once that is over, Gabriel for some reason gravitates out to the landing, where Mary Jane and Gretta are attempting to convince Molly to stay for supper. When she declines and seems destined to escape, he offers to walk her home, obviously envious of her flight, although he must realize that he is required at the dinner table. The dinner itself is a comic opera of mistimings; Gabriel, although having to be called in to carve, officiates at this rite with the utmost self-confidence ("He felt quite at ease now for he was an expert carver"), but loses out on the first round of food, carving "second helpings as soon as he had finished the first round without serving himself" (De 197). Both the figure at the head of the table and a voluntary outcast from the feast ("kindly forget my existence," he insists – De 198), he momentarily loses himself in eating. Meanwhile the "dance" goes on around him:

> Aunt Kate and Aunt Julia were still toddling round the table, walking on each other's heels, getting in each other's way and giving each other unheeded orders. Mr Browne begged them to sit down and eat their supper and so did Gabriel but they said there was time enough so that, at last, Freddy Malins stood up and, capturing Aunt Kate, plumped her down on her chair amid general laughter.   (De 197–8)

Gabriel's speech and the finalizing toast form the fluctuating individuals into a cohesive unit at last, as "the singers turned towards one another, as if in melodious conference" (De 205), only to result in the final dispersal of the guests out into the night.

Gabriel's crises of identity plague him throughout the evening and pursue him into the culminating revelations in the darkened hotel room. To Lily he is "Mister Con-o-roy" ("he smiled at the three syllables she had given his surname" – De 177); to Kate and Julia Morkan he is "their favourite nephew" (De 179), yet he later judges himself as "acting as a pennyboy for his aunts" (De 220); and his conjunction with Freddy Malins (whom Browne calls Teddy) much too closely identifies him with that ludicrous figure. For himself he prefers the persona of "C.G.", the book reviewer, a semi-secret self that can be found wandering the quays haunting the bookshops, but the reviews are written for the *Daily Express*, so that Molly Ivors is able to unmask him and identify him as a "West Briton" (De 190). Even deeper in Gabriel's storehouse of secret identities, however, is someone that a Miss Devlin would recognize as a "romantic person", an identity that has remained for too long in hiding and motivates Gabriel as he brings Gretta into his arena of sexual passion in the Gresham hotel room. But two romantic persons cannot occupy the same space in Gretta's memory, and the arena belongs now to Michael Furey, relegating Gabriel Conroy to the persona of a retroactive cuckold.

The death of his romantic self that evolves from Gretta's resurrection of Michael Furey ("the evocation of this figure from the dead") causes Gabriel to brood on his newly realized lack of personal identity, which takes the form of conjuring up and labelling a multitude of multiple identities until now secreted away under those other misleading headings:

> While he had been full of memories of their secret life together, she had been comparing him in her mind with another. A shameful consciousness of his own person assailed him. He saw himself as a ludicrous figure, acting as a pennyboy for his aunts, a nervous well-meaning sentimentalist, orating to vulgarians and idealising his own clownish lusts, the pitiable fatuous fellow he had caught a glimpse of in the mirror.   (De 219–20)

It is the death of Gabriel Conroy that is being enacted in the closing moments of "The Dead", which he attempts to hold at bay by substitution, knowing that he must have a death to replace that of his own self. His awareness that "some impalpable and vindictive being was coming against him, gathering forces against him in its vague world" (De 220) – to the boy in "The Sisters" paralysis sounded "like the name of some maleficent and sinful being" (Si 9) – is not assuaged by dwelling upon the Furey grave in far Oughterard: one much closer to home would be that of Aunt Julia, and he proceeds to gratuitously dig her grave. Of the two aunts she is the younger, described at first as "quite grey", although Kate is "too feeble to go about much" (De 176). At a second glance it is seen that "her slow eyes and parted lips gave her the appearance of a woman who did not know where she was or where she was going", and Kate's face is seen as "healthier than her sister's" (De 179). Gabriel is present at the second instance and might well have made his choice for a sacrificial victim from that observation. He now needs to see himself as the surviving mourner, and a culminating context verifies his sense of her impending demise: on 16 June 1904 Stephen Dedalus will think "of his grandmother Miss Kate Morkan in the house of her dying sister Miss Julia Morkan at 15

Usher's Island" (It 139–41).

Loss of personal identity, however, is unavoidable for any of those who manufacture a false identity for themselves, attempting to satisfy pathetic needs by sailing under false colours. A boy who sees himself as a knight errant bearing a chalice in a Dublin market place is destined to realize himself derided by vanity, and a young woman who fancies herself a lass loved by a sailor will turn to stone when she anticipates the moment of ascension into flight. (However, as the verdict in "A Painful Case" attests, "No blame attached to anyone".) In the dark nights of their souls James Duffy and Gabriel Conroy find themselves on a parallel course, bound to each other by a death and a love, unaware of their mutual plight. In Phoenix Park Duffy is conscious that "the prostrate creatures down by the wall were watching him and wished him gone" (Pa 117); in his hotel room Gabriel is aware that "Other forms were near. His soul approached that region where dwell the vast hosts of the dead. He was conscious of, but could not apprehend, their wayward and flickering existence" (De 223). Just as Duffy acknowledges that "One human being had seemed to love him", and that "venal and furtive loves filled him with despair" (Pa 117), Gabriel knows that "he had never felt like that himself towards any woman but he knew that such a feeling must be love" (De 223). And in each case the absent ghost subsumes and dissipates the presumed identity of the one incapable of love: Duffy "began to doubt the reality of what memory told him" so that he "could not feel her near him in the darkness" (Pa 117); Gabriel "in the partial darkness . . . imagined he saw the form of a young man standing under a dripping tree", but "his own identity was fading out into a grey impalpable world" (De 223). The death of the self consumed James Duffy when he knew irrevocably that "he was alone" (Pa 117), and Gabriel Conroy confronts the realization that he will "fade and wither dismally with age" (De 223). Collective identity now seems to exist for him with "all the living and the dead" (De 224), while his individual identity has come to be devoid of any real substance. The insistent assurance of selfhood that was at the core of Stephen Dedalus's being towards the end of *A Portrait* has no corollary in *Dubliners*, a multiple narrative that makes its linear inroads into *Ulysses*, but also foreshadows the annihilation of compact individuality in the discontinuous text of *Finnegans Wake*, where all possibilities are open and active.

Index

25